D1554799

O Ye Legendary Texas Horned Frog!

31 YEARS INSIDE THE CORNERSTONE OF THE EASTLAND COUNTY COURTHOUSE,

O YE

Legendary

Texas

HORNED

frog

AND OTHER HORNED TOAD TALES.

OLD RIP, WHO SLEPT

June Rayfield Welch

Copyright 1993

by

June Rayfield Welch

Library of Congress Catalog Card Number
93-60217

ISBN 0-912854-17-0

YELLOW
R·O·S·E
P·R·E·S·S

Box 140221 • Irving, Texas 75014

For Ryan, whose world

should include some horny toads

and other old Texas things.

— Texas Christian University

A classic study of a Texas Horned Lizard.

Contents

Illustrations

Preface

To live in Texas in my time was to know the horny toad as part of the friends and furniture of the world. I wrote about Eastland's Old Rip in an earlier book, but there is more to be said in gratitude for the contributions those splendidly ugly little creatures made to my early years. Horned frogs roamed the grounds of Benjamin Franklin Elementary School in Gainesville and inhabited the vacant lot beside our home.

Unlike most of my contemporaries, I do not have a horned frog story of my own. While researching this book I asked everyone I encountered about his last sighting of a horned frog. The informant's demeanor always changed; he or she would smile, ruminate, and share a relevant memory. But I can recall no single episode that would adequately suggest the emotions the fierce-looking creatures provoked. Fortunately, an old friend—completely unaware that I needed a good horned frog tale—supplied the deficiency. Mrs. Myrtle Weems Shelton wrote to my mother:

> At our old home place in Brownwood my mother had a large vegetable garden out back. She found a large horn frog in her garden. She saw him every time she entered the garden. She wondered if he had anything to eat, so she started carrying him large red ants. Her three grandsons living in the country started carrying jars of ants to her. She said if she was a little slow putting the

ants down to him he would crawl onto the toe of her shoe and look up to her. She loved that horn frog and it brought tears to my eyes when I heard about him. Later I wished I had asked her what happened to her pet. I do know for several years she fed him.[1]

I have not seen a live horny toad in a quarter century. They seem to be scarce east of Fort Worth—the home of Texas Christian University's Fighting Frogs.[2] Even west of Tarrant County the toad population is negligible when compared with the numbers of fifty years ago.

Because much of the Texas citizenry is urban, young, and domiciled east of the 98th meridian—and because many residents moved to the state as adults from more Northern climes—the majority of Texans probably have never seen a horny toad. Appalled by this unfortunate situation, some great souls have recently formed The Horned Lizard Conservation Society to assist the toads' return to health and prosperity. That organization's burgeoning membership kindles hopes for an early revival of the horned frog in large numbers throughout the state.

---

1 Myrtle Weems Shelton, Houston, Texas, to Elzina Prigmore Welch, Brownwood, Texas, October 9, 1992.

2 Athletic teams were named for the toads inhabiting the T. C. U. campus at Waco. Baylor University Biology Professor Fred Gehlbach reported that few sightings of horned frogs had been made in McLennan County since the early 1980s.

This slender volume makes no attempt to settle such important questions as the longevity of Eastland's Old Rip. It aspires only to celebrate that durable friend of the old Texans—the horny toad—and to preserve a tiny slice of history and folklore that helps explain, among other things, why the desiccated body of a Texas Horned Lizard occupies a show window in the front wall of the Eastland County courthouse—lying in state for the edification of believers and skeptics alike, a West Texas Lenin—and still influences the life and commerce of the community.[3]

———

I am indebted to Ann Huey-Bishop for the cover art, the horned frog design, the map, and the drawings of Coolidge, House, and Truman. Marie Giles Chalk and Lynda Chalk Welch edited the manuscript, and Cyndi Wendt Sykora made a book out of it, for all of which I am grateful.

June Rayfield Welch
University of Dallas
Irving, Texas

---

[3] A happy consequence of recent world events is the possible need to explain this reference, for the USSR's demise may portend removal of the body of founder Nicolai Lenin from the great tomb in Moscow's Red Square, where it has been displayed the past seven decades.

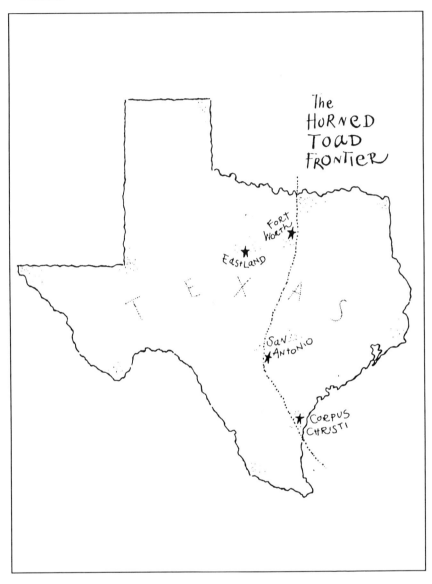

The
HoRNeD
ToaD
FRoNTieR

FORT
WoRTH ★

★ EastLaND

T E X A S

San
★ AntoNio

★ CoRPUS
CHRISTI

— *Ann Huey-Bishop*

Although the Texas Horned Lizard was found throughout the state in
former times, by 1992 much of the population had been lost and horny
toads were almost non-existent east of this line.

Of Horny Toads And Texans

Visitors to Texas have always been fascinated by horned frogs. When Dr. Ferdinand Von Roemer, a German lawyer and paleontologist, arrived to survey the mineral resources of the Republic, he was impressed by the beguiling horny toad.[4]

In 1845, Dr. Roemer observed no large game on Galveston Island, although he learned that once deer had been plentiful. Except for a few recently-planted ornamental varieties, only three trees—all live oaks—grew on the island. But of the numerous toads, he wrote:

> The so-called horned frog (*Phrynosoma orbiculare Wiegm*)[5] member of the reptile family, is also an object of much interest to the newly arrived European, since no animal in Europe resembles it. It is a lizard, about a span long, whose broad, stiff, thorny projections on the back of the head give it a peculiar and formidable appearance.

---

4 Sponsored by the Berlin Academy of Sciences—and bearing a letter of introduction from renowned scientist Baron Alexander Von Humboldt, a good friend of Thomas Jefferson—Roemer, in his late twenties, traveled Texas from 1845 to 1847.

5 Actually, the scientific name for the Texas Horned Lizard is *Phrynosoma Cornutum.*

These harmless creatures were very plentiful in the gardens of Galveston. A boy, whom I had commissioned in the morning to capture some, brought me a dozen in the afternoon.[6]

Informed writers always point out that the horned frog is misnamed. It is not a frog. Neither is the creature a toad, although it stalks prey in toad-fashion: an unsuspecting red ant—oblivious to any danger—after a flick of the lizard's tongue, suddenly finds itself on the menu.[7]

The Texas Horned Lizard—a relative of the iguana—is quite shy. In an emergency it scampers away and hides. On the other hand, the bold South American horned frog—the genuine article—eats anything, mice, insects, each other. A true frog, "complete with tadpoles," the Latin American reptile would "hang on like a bulldog." Texas Christian University professor Gary Ferguson explained that

They've been known to chomp grazing horses on the lip, and some ranchers claim the horses have died from the wound, possibly from the infection. They also can give people a nasty bite.[8]

---

6 Ferdinand Roemer, *Texas*, San Antonio, Texas: Standard Printing Company, 1935, 41. In his book, first published in Bonn, Germany in 1849, Roemer stated that he saw none of the toads during his tour of "Western Texas"; however, he visited only a small part of West Texas, where, in 1992, the main horned frog population lived.

7 Doris Cochran, "When Is A Toad Not a Toad?", *Nature,* January 1932. A Texas Horned Lizard lives on insects—particularly red ants, which constitute 50% of its diet—while toads consume worms and similar goodies.

8 *TCU Monthly*, October 1975.

When Lawrence Curtis—a former director of the Fort Worth Zoo—referred to Texas Christian University's mascot as a horned lizard and advocated the use of its proper name, *Dallas News* columnist Frank Tolbert joined issue. Tolbert's spirited defense of traditional "horned frog" nomenclature included quotation of this less-than-memorable poem written by his friend S. Omar Barker—"Old S. O. B."—who was then the poet laureate of New Mexico:

The horny toad, ill-graced, but harmless,
Is thought by some to be quite charmless.
At least he helps eat garden ants up
And does not try to crawl your pants up.

Tolbert also presented—with approval, although certainly not with pride—the poetic rejoinder of a ficticious Miss Imogene Twitty, of Bog, Nacogdoches County:

That Professor Curtis may be a science wizard
But he'll not make me call a horned frog a lizard.[9]

Horned frogs are found from southwestern Canada throughout the western half of the United States and Mexico. Their habitat ranges from sea level to elevations of 9,000 feet, and they exist mainly in arid regions.[10]

Of three species native to this state, the Texas Horned Lizard is the most widely distributed. It also

---

9   *Dallas Morning News*, April 5, 1967.
10   *Encyclopedia Americana*, Vol. 14, 386.

inhabits parts of Louisiana, Oklahoma, Kansas, Colorado, New Mexico, Arizona, and Mexico. *Phrynosoma Cornutum*—the scientific name for the creature—translates as "horned toad body." An adult measures from 3 to 5 inches in length and has a broad, flat torso, a short tail, and a pointed snout. Its color varies according to the soil, from light brown to tan or gray.[11]

The crown of spines on the back of the lizard's head includes two large center spikes that give the appearance of horns. Although the lizard does not use the points aggressively, the spines do discourage enemies, and they constitute defensive weapons. Jim Goins wrote that,

> Predators find the horned lizard more than a mouthful as it twists, turns and arches its head, driving home these points on the attacker. Snakes sometimes swallow horned lizards, not realizing it may be their last meal.[12]

The horned frog inhabits flat, open, dry country with little plant cover except for bunchgrass and cactus, and seeks shelter under rocks, among low-growing vegetation, or in burrows of other animals. Using head, limbs, and ribs, the toad digs itself a place in sand or rocky soil.[13]

---

11 Dennis Campbell, "Backyard and Beyond," *Dallas Morning News,* September 13, 1981.

12 *Texas Parks & Wildlife,* Vol. 50, No. 8, August 1992, 33.

13 Judith M. Garrett, and David G. Barker, *A Field Guide to Reptiles & Amphibians of Texas*, Austin: Texas Monthly Press, 1987, 152.

Not endowed with the speed of many other lizards, the horny toad is active only during the daytime. At night the reptile chooses a safe place and "literally sinks from sight as it makes lateral, scooping motions with its body until only the top of the head remains above the surface of the soil."[14]

Even though the horned frog lives within an area of only 100 to 200 square yards, it requires a base of about 20 acres because red ants constitute the bulk of the diet and their beds are scattered.

The toad has a body temperature of 105 degrees. It adapts easily to heat and cold because of the insulation provided by the short, flat body, which absorbs much of the sun's heat. They are seen only in late spring and summer—spreading their bodies and tilting toward the sun's rays. Lower temperatures force the lizards to hibernate underground from September or October to late April or early May.[15]

Mating occurs soon after hibernation ends. The female digs a hole five to seven inches deep into which she lays about thirty eggs. Depending upon ground temperature, incubation lasts from five and a half to seven weeks.

---

14 Campbell, *Dallas Morning News.*
15 Garrett, *Field Guide*, 153.

Hatchlings measure just over an inch from nose to tail. Horned lizards usually live about three years.

The toad's main protection consists of blending into the background. A thorny appearance and camouflage coloration help. In case of discovery, a horny toad makes a serious effort to intimidate the enemy. The creature can inflate itself to almost twice normal size and appears to be dangerous. Under extreme stress the toad flattens its body and can shoot a stream of blood a distance of three feet as an eyelid ruptures under pressure. (The object is to blind an opponent temporarily.) The toad's eye returns to normal within minutes.[16]

As Dr. Ferguson described the process, the horned frog's first daily chore is to heat its blood. Early in the morning the toad peers out of the sand or soil and blood flowing to the head is heated by the sun's rays. (Exposing only the head serves the purpose and provides more safety from predators than complete exposure.) In an emergency, "the blood squirts out of their eyes, they squeeze them so tight."[17]

16 Boyce House, *Cowtown Columnist*, San Antonio, Texas: The Naylor Company, 1946, 8.

17 *TCU Monthly*, October 1975.

This metal sculpture presides over the Fort Worth campus of Texas Christian University, which adopted the horned frog as the symbol of its athletic teams because of the fierce appearance and durability of the reptiles and because they were so plentiful on the Waco campus. The 1938 Horned Frogs were the first Texas team to win a national collegiate football championship, and their 145-pound quarterback, David O'Brien, won the Heisman Trophy.

— Ann Huey-Bishop

Among admirers of the horny toad was Harry S Truman, of Missouri, whose Texas cousin sent a pair to him in a matchbox.

Harry Truman And Other Horned Frog Fanciers

A widespread interest in the Texas Horned Lizard and belief in its extraordinary powers of endurance was suggested by a letter young Harry S Truman sent to classmate—and future wife—Bess Wallace. From Grandview, Missouri, on May 23, 1911, the future president wrote:

Dear Bessie:

Mary's (mine also) cousin in Texas sent her two horned toads in a box by mail the other day. She thought it was a box of pills. It was all wrapped up and very small. You ought to have heard her squawk when she opened the box. You know they have tails and horns on their heads (their tails are not on their heads) and are furious looking little brutes, but are harmless. They feast on flies, ants, etc. I don't see how these two lived, for the the box was air-tight.[18]

Truman's pride of ownership was not unique. Their popularity was a threat to the horny toads' future. Capture

---

18 Robert H. Ferrell, Ed., *Dear Bess*, New York: W. W. Norton & Company, 1983, 35. Harry S Truman wrote these letters to Bess Wallace between 1910 and 1959.

and sale of the little beasts may have hastened them along the path toward extinction.

As Assistant Attorney General Bert Cox helped organize an association to protect the horned frogs, he recalled that, as a boy, he could have mowed his Abilene yard much faster and with less difficulty if it had not been necessary to stop frequently and move toads out of harm's way. Illustrating the frogs' broad attraction, Cox told of a profitable sojourn at a national Boy Scout Jamboree in Valley Forge, Pennsylvania:

> The horny toads were about the finest trading material we had. I got an Indian Headdress, a fancy bullwhip and a fancy Hawaiian lei. Just fabulous stuff, all traded for a shoe box of horned toads I'd picked up in about a half hour.[19]

A few decades ago—deploring the negative consequences of their seemingly universal appeal—Wayne McAlister stated,

> Almost every traveler who visits Texas returns home with a shoe box under his arm which contains an odd little creature known widely as the Texas horned toad. For, along with the diamondback rattler and the coyote, this lively little reptile has become an animated symbol of Texas and the Southwest.[20]

---

19 *Dallas Times Herald*, January 16, 1990.
20 Wayne McAlister, "Horned Symbol of Texas," *Texas Game and Fish*, 1953.

Because of its popularity and the ease with which it may be captured, the horned lizard is often kept in captivity by many travelers and other interested persons. Unfortunately many people are ignorant of the little animal's necessities and the pets often die from various avoidable causes.

Horned lizards live rather well in captivity if they are given the proper attention. A necessity in keeping these little reptiles successfully is a roomy cage with a few inches of dry sand on the bottom and several objects under which the pet may crawl. Sunshine should be available, but some shade must always be on hand. Mealworms, ants, and other live insects may be offered for food. Occasionally the interior of the cage should be finely sprinkled with water. Of course, a warm temperature should be provided.

Another West Texan, author Carlton Stowers, was heavily involved in the horny toad traffic. As a sixth grader, he shipped thousands of the lizards from Ballinger.[21] On the way home from school he would search vacant lots and alleys for ant beds that would attract toads in season. Stowers said,

> I got an address from somewhere, maybe a magazine, about a curio shop in Topeka and they said they'd pay 10 cents for big ones and a nickel apiece for little ones. I guess they figured a kid from Hackensack, New Jersey would want a horned toad for a pet over a bullfrog

---

21 Carlton Stowers, of Cedar Hill, won the 1985 Edgar Allan Poe award for his book *Careless Whispers.*

or a lizard. Anyway, it was like a job for me. I was
rolling in dough, making maybe $20 a week.[22]

Resisting pressure by friends who wanted the buyer's
name and address, Stowers guarded his secret carefully.
Business increased, and

> Then I got the idea of hiring other kids to collect
> them. I paid three cents apiece for the frogs and sold 'em
> for a dime. I put people to work.

From his inventory—stored in a No. 2 washtub—Stowers
made regular weekly shipments of toads to Kansas.

Horned lizards—tough, proud, and fierce in appearance and bearing—were so plentiful on Texas Christian
University's old Waco campus that students adopted them
as mascots and appropriated their name for athletic teams.
The undefeated, Sugar Bowl champion, 1938 Horned Frogs
were the first Southwest Conference representative to win
a national collegiate football title, and quarterback David
O'Brien, the 145-pound All-American, was Texas' first
Heisman trophy winner.

Horned toads were regularly held as pets by young
Texans. They were good luck charms. Small boys—who
had little more to bet than marbles and string—raced them.
But some uses may have been overlooked. Midwestern

---

22 *Dallas Morning News*, June 7, 1992.

farm boys, who made baseballs of straw and mud stuffed inside a cowhide cover, liked to put a dead frog at the center to give bounce to the finished product. Had the practice extended to Texas, the preferred core might well have been one of the plentiful horny toads.[23]

Celebrated hat designer Lily Dache became a devotee of horny toads after reading about Old Rip. When her millinery company erected a six-story building near the Drake Hotel in New York City, Miss Dache considered it requisite to the success of the enterprise to entomb a live horned frog in the cornerstone. Mrs. Leonard Hall—the wife of the congressman who was then the national chairman of the Republican party—obtained a Texas Horned Lizard for Miss Dache. She deposited the toad in the stone along with such memorabilia as the first hat she ever designed. Well into construction of the building, two men posing as representatives of the Society for Prevention of Cruelty to Animals demanded freedom for the toad. Miss Dache ordered the cornerstone broken open and the frog liberated. Mrs. Hall then confessed that the men were imposters who were helping perpetrate a hoax she had concocted out of sympathy for the horned toad she had helped to condemn. As a peace offering—in order to close the episode and make amends for any wounded feelings—Mrs. Hall gave the famous maker of women's hats an

---

23 W. P. Kinsella, *Shoeless Joe*, Boston: Houghton-Mifflin Publishing Company, 1982.

expensive glass case for the lizard, which graduated from prisoner to pet. Lily Dache wrote, "My ancient, wise, good-luck horned toad now lives in his glass palace in my penthouse."[24]

While scientists taught that the life span of horned frogs was only three or four years, many old West Texans believed they could endure a century or more without food, water, or air. Everyone had heard stories about their survival for incredible periods in states of suspended animation. The common wisdom in Texas would dictate that finally—as confidence in the scientific method increased—someone would perform an experiment to test the endurance of horny frogs.

---

24 *Dallas Morning News*, October 29, 1970.

Eastland's County Clerk
Tested A Texas Belief

Just as the City of West is not located in West Texas, Eastland is situated far from East Texas. Created just before the beginning of the Civil War, Eastland County—in West Central Texas—is about 100 miles west of Fort Worth.

The county bears the name of Texas hero William Mosby Eastland, who was born in Woodford County, Kentucky on March 21, 1806 and grew up in Tennessee. At General Edward Burleson's suggestion, Eastland moved to Texas and settled near La Grange in 1834. Under the command of Colonel John H. Moore, Eastland served in Indian campaigns against the Waco and Tawakoni, and soon after he fought in the battle of San Jacinto, Eastland became a Ranger captain. [25]

In early 1842, General Raphael Vasquez led a 500-man army north from Mexico to San Antonio. Vasquez soon withdrew, but Texians were shaken by the knowledge

---

25 W. P. Webb, Ed., *The Handbook of Texas*, Austin: The Texas State Historical Association, 1952, Vol. 1, 538.

that Mexican troops could invade the new country at will and without attracting attention until too late. The Congress of the Republic of Texas tried to appropriate $50,000 for offensive operations against Mexico; however, the treasury was without funds.

On September 1 of that same year, General Adrian Woll marched into San Antonio with artillery and a thousand Mexican troops. Retreating, Woll took with him into captivity 53 Texians—the judge, lawyers, litigants, and witnesses who had been present at a Bexar County district court trial. As news of the raid spread over Texas, a punitive expedition was authorized to retaliate against Mexico. At La Grange, William Eastland raised a company that became part of the army commanded by General Alexander Somervell.

At the Rio Grande, General Somervell halted the march, disbanded the force, and ordered a return to the Texas settlements. Many of the men objected. Having endured many hardships without seeing any military action, about 300 resentful volunteers decided to continue the effort to discourage armed trespassers upon Texas soil. Under the command of William S. Fisher they would invade Mexico.[26]

---

26 Fisher County is named for him; Roby is the seat of government. The original movement was called the Somervell Expedition and this campaign was the Mier Expedition.

Captain Eastland commanded one of the six companies that made up the new expedition. Crossing the Rio Grande, the Texians fought well in the old town of Mier on Christmas Day, but—for some strange reason—Colonel Fisher surrendered to General Pedro Ampudia. The Texians were tied in pairs and marched to prison deep inside Mexico.[27]

After an attempted mass escape at Hacienda Salado, about a hundred miles below Saltillo, General Antonio Lopez de Santa Anna—of Alamo, Goliad, and San Jacinto notoriety—ordered every recaptured prisoner to be shot. Governor Francisco Mexia refused to obey, and Santa Anna amended his decree to require the execution of every tenth man. Into an earthen jar Mexican officers placed 159 white—and 17 black—beans. Each of the blindfolded Texians was required to take a bean from the container. Those who drew black ones were shot.[28] William Eastland was the first to choose a black bean, and at Hacienda Salado, he and the other condemned prisoners were seated on a log and shot at sunset on March 25, 1843. Five years

---

27 George B. Erath, *The Memoirs of Major George B. Erath, 1813-1891*, Waco: The Heritage Society of Waco, 1956. One of two Texian prisoners who managed to escape from Mier after the surrender was Whitfield Chalk, the great-great-grandfather of my wife, Lynda Chalk Welch.

28 James M. Day, *Black Beans and Goose Quills*, Waco: Texian Press, 1970. William Alexander "Bigfoot" Wallace realized that the beans were different in size and was able to select a white one. The survivors were walked to Castle Perote prison, where Texians captured at San Antonio by General Woll also were confined.

later, their remains were moved to Monument Hill near La Grange, Fayette County.[29]

———

In the 1860 federal census, Eastland County had only 99 residents—mostly stock farmers. When the county was organized—thirteen years later—the seat of government, Merriman, was only the headquarters of Flannegan's Ranch. Merriman had no suitable building in which to conduct the public business; furthermore, the capital was not located within five miles of the heart of the county, as Texans preferred. Officials lived elsewhere and kept the public records at their homes. The district court convened at Alameda in a two-story log cabin—the only structure in Eastland County large enough for the purpose. "Even then the Grand Jury had to hold its sessions under the nearby trees."[30]

Since Merriman showed negligible growth potential and was not centrally located—as the law intended—Charles U. Connellee and J. S. Daugherty, in late 1874, platted the town of Eastland on a 320-acre tract near the heart of the county. Hoping to make their village the seat of government, the promoters built a rock house with space

———

29 Webb, *Handbook of Texas*, Vol. 2, 189-190.

30 Edwin T. Cox, *History of Eastland County*, San Antonio: Naylor Company, 1950, 30.

on the second story for a courtroom and offices. That building was the county capitol for eight years. Connellee and Daugherty granted a 200-foot by 200-foot tract for use as the public square.[31] In an election to relocate the county seat, Eastland polled 67 votes to only nine for Merriman. Eastland town lots were sold to pay for a city prison, which Eastland County's stationery advertised as "The finest jail west of Fort Worth."[32]

The hamlet of Cisco was established at the intersection of the tracks of the Texas and Pacific Railway and the Missouri, Kansas, and Texas Railroad. Cisco boosters immediately began trying to acquire the county government. In an 1881 election, Eastland polled only 354 votes, while upstart Cisco received 324. Frightened businessmen acted quickly to anchor the government in Eastland. A native stone courthouse was completed on the public square in 1883. Since the county was still indebted for part of the construction cost, the Eastlanders were confident. Taxpayers were not likely to change the location while the courthouse was new and encumbered. (A move to Cisco would mean abandoning a perfectly good capitol, erecting another, and obliging the taxpayers to pay the principal and interest on two sets of bonds.)

---

31 Pearl Ghormley, *Eastland County, Texas*, Austin: Rupegy Publishing Company, 1969, 21.

32 *West Texas Historical Association Yearbook*, 1930, 140. Cox, *Eastland County*, 31.

When Eastland's courthouse burned in 1896, a wooden temple of justice was erected to forestall Cisco's ambitions. Cisco citizens saw the situation as a splendid opportunity to acquire the county offices, and another election was called in 1897. Cisco drew 940 ballots to Eastland's 553, but the courthouse remained in Eastland. Because Cisco was more than five miles from the center of the county, it needed a two-thirds vote to prevail.

Confirmed as the county seat, Eastland was free to build a new capitol. Some claim that construction of that fourth courthouse was the most important event in Eastland County history.[33] The commissioners issued $5,000 worth of courthouse and jail bonds on May 14, 1897, and contracted to build a $49,000 capitol. (Insurance proceeds from the courthouse fire supplied the other $44,000.)[34]

On the day the cornerstone of the new courthouse was to be leveled—July 19, 1897—County Clerk Ernest E. Wood went home, two blocks from the square, for lunch.[35] As he started back to work Wood noticed his little boy, Will, playing with a horny toad, and he was reminded of a recent newspaper story about a dormant frog discovered inside a rock in East Texas. Wood decided to test the old Texan belief that a horned frog could live indefinitely in a place

---

33 Cox, *Eastland County*, 32-33.

34 The brick temple of justice was completed in 1898.

35 In my time, this was called dinner; supper was the evening meal. Lunch consisted of edibles carried in a brown sack or a metal box to work or school.

from which light and air had been excluded. He took the lizard with him.[36] Since Wood played cornet in the band that was to perform at the leveling ceremonies, he had to get someone else to drop the toad inside the cornerstone. [37]

After his term ended, County Clerk Wood went into the abstract business. In 1936 he became Justice of the Peace and performed 1,600 weddings before his death on April 3, 1952.[38]

Wood's decision to drop the lizard into the cornerstone changed the future of Eastland County and eventually yielded a unique tourist site—a mausoleum not so grand as the one occupied by the remains of Nicolai Lenin in Moscow's Red Square and in which the incumbent was no statesman, soldier, or politician but an ordinary, dried-up, Texas horny toad.

---

36 Interview of Mrs. Will Wood in Abilene, September 29, 1979. Mrs. Wood, at age six, was present when the cornerstone was sealed. She did not see what was placed inside but knew that the contents included her mother's Bible. Mrs. Wood was among the spectators thirty-one years later when Rip was removed. *Dallas Morning News*, February 22, 1928.

37 House, *Cowtown Columnist*, 3-4. Jim Golden stated that Will Wood had put the frog in the stone; however, Wood was only four years old in 1897.

38 *History of Eastland County*, 600.

The present Eastland County temple of justice, built in 1928, towers over downtown Eastland.

The Nation Watched The Opening
Of A West Texas Cornerstone

Nineteen hundred twenty-seven was a memorable year. One day Calvin Coolidge called in reporters and handed them strips of paper on which was written, "I do not choose to run for President in 1928."[39] A week later Coolidge became an honorary Sioux chief and was crowned with a war bonnet made of 200 feathers. The president was welcomed by nineteen aged warriors who had helped defeat George Armstrong Custer and the Seventh Cavalry half a century before.[40] That year Babe Ruth hit sixty home runs—setting a record that endured until Roger Maris got sixty-one in 1961.[41] But the biggest story in 1927— by far—was the solo flight to France of young Charles Lindbergh. With supplies consisting of four sandwiches and two canteens of water, Lindbergh took off in *The Spirit of St. Louis* from Roosevelt Field, Long Island, New York

---

39 *Time*, August 8, 1927. Coolidge's stenographer typed the statement several times, then cut the pages into strips. Reporters were summoned, and Coolidge handed each reporter a slip bearing the ten words. He refused to say more.

40 *Time*, August 15, 1927.

41 *Time*, October 10, 1927.

and landed at Le Bourget Airport, in France, after 33 hours, 29 minutes and 3,600 miles.[42]

Now, in February 1928, an ordinary civic function in West Texas produced a figure to share the stage with Coolidge and Lindbergh. The 1897 Eastland County courthouse had been razed after three decades of hard use during which substantial changes had occurred in Texas.

The mighty Spindletop gusher had exploded into being at Beaumont on the tenth day of the new century. Heavy crude oil from the Jefferson County well shot through the top of the derrick and continued at a daily volume of nearly 100,000 barrels. Nine days were required to stop the flow and cap the well. (The state's total petroleum production had been only 900,000 barrels in all of the preceding year—1900.) After four more gushers were drilled, the Spindletop field was outproducing the rest of the nation. As Mayor Samuel M. "Golden Rule" Jones, of Toledo, Ohio, put it, the ocean of oil promised by Jefferson County's production meant that petroleum was destined to be the fuel of the twentieth century.

Oil fever swept Texas. Paying quantities of petroleum were discovered at Burkburnett and elsewhere in West Texas, but the most spectacular strike occurred in 1917 near

---

42 *Time*, May 30, 1927. Lindbergh averaged 107 1/2 miles an hour. In 1926 Raymond Orteig had offered $25,000 to the first person who flew nonstop from New York to France. Lindbergh was only one of many who hoped to win the prize.

Ranger, in Eastland County. Located near an old Texas Rangers campsite, the village of Ranger experienced little growth until the McCleskey discovery well came in. Almost overnight the population swelled from a few hundred to 40,000 or 50,000, and in 1919 the Ranger field produced 22 million barrels of oil.

The gusher on John McClesky's farm erupted just at the time when oil was most in demand. World War I was expanding and petroleum might make the difference between victory and defeat.[43] Trading in leases and land sales generated a massive increase in legal business, and by 1928 the Eastland courthouse was worn out, used up, and outgrown.

Despite an overwhelming compulsion to get rich— in which most Texans seemed to share—the Merriman Cemetery earned a reputation as the "graveyard that was not for sale." Every effort to drill oil wells on the premises was rebuffed by relatives of the pioneers buried there. Derricks and producing wells surrounded—but were never permitted to invade—the cemetery.[44]

The Ranger boom attracted all kinds of people to Eastland County. Rex Beach came to gather material for

---

43 A month after the Armistice, Lord Curzon declared, "American oil, and hardly any other, made up that 'wave of petroleum' on which the war was won." James Presley, *A Saga of Wealth*, New York: G. P. Putnam's Sons, 1978, 97.

44 Harry Hansen, Ed., *Texas, A Guide to the Lone Star State*, New York: Hastings House, 1969, 539-540.

his book *Flowing Gold*. Evangelist Billy Sunday preached to a street crowd of 5,000. Former president William Howard Taft lectured one evening, and promoter "Tex" Rickard brought heavyweight champion Jess Willard to town. At nearby Cisco, Conrad Hilton purchased the Mobley Hotel—the first in his far-flung empire of Hilton hotels that finally would include the Waldorf-Astoria in Manhattan. Renting beds twice in each 24 hours, Hilton described the Mobley as a "cross between a gold mine and a flop house."[45]

Ranger's railroad freight volume in 1919 totaled more than receipts in Dallas, Fort Worth, and New Orleans combined. But the Ranger Field's reserves declined rapidly as ruinous competition resulted in the drilling of too many wells. Wasted gas depleted the energy of the reservoir and left trapped a lake of petroleum.[46]

Most Eastland residents were aware that Justice of the Peace Ernest Wood was supposed to have caused a horned frog to be sealed inside the cornerstone of the brick courthouse. Many old timers looked forward to the eventual demolition of that temple of justice in order to satisfy their curiosity or justify their statements about horny toad longevity. Then, in that special year of 1927, the courthouse was condemned and ordered torn down.[47]

---

45 Presley, *Saga*, 94.

46 Presley, *Saga*, 96-97.

47 House, *Cowtown Columnist*, 4.

Well aware that small town skeletons tend to tumble out of closets, Wood may have calculated that his actions would be best accepted if he were the narrator, so he told many newcomers about the horned frog in the cornerstone. When Railway Express agent H. A. McCanlies moved to Eastland, in 1921, he rented a house from Wood. Smarting under the criticism he had suffered over the years, Wood explained his part in the imprisonment of the toad. McCanlies said, "He, like myself and other folks, had always heard that a horned frog would live a hundred years or more if it could find an airtight space."[48]

Wood also informed *Eastland Argus-Tribune* editor Boyce House. When the old courthouse was slated for demolition the excited newpaperman informed his readers that questions about the entombed lizard would soon be answered. Picked up by the wire services, the Eastland horny toad story appeared in newspapers throughout the nation and beyond the seas. As interest grew and suspense increased, House wrote additional pieces. Pleased by the space he was given by other journals, the editor wrote, "The Eastland frog became the most famous animal since the serpent in the Garden of Eden."[49] House compared the toad's

---

48 Clipping dated April 2, 1972 from an unidentified newspaper taped to a wall in the Eastland County Clerk's office..

49 Ghormley, *Eastland County*, 165.

publicity to that generated by Lindbergh's lonely flight to France a few months earlier.[50]

On Saturday, February 18, 1928, at least 1,500—perhaps more than 2,000—Texans gathered at Eastland's public square to observe the cornerstone opening.[51] Witnesses crowded the square and the streets; they perched on piles of debris and fragments of the old building; they peered from office windows and rooftops. Ernest Wood called out, "If there is a horned frog in there, it's mine."

Suddenly, House was apprehensive. In fact, he was badly frightened, for he would be the butt of heavy-handed and long-lasting ridicule if the cornerstone held no frog or evidence that one had sojourned there. House feared that the toad's body had long ago turned to dust. He would be grateful for any sign of the lizard's occupancy. He wrote,

> A jagged wall of brick, eight feet high, still stood above the stone. A chain was looped about the wall and a truck (to which the chain was attached) began to pull. So firmly was the wall cemented to the cornerstone that not only the wall but also the stone began to yield.

---

50 House, *Cowtown Columnist*, 4. *Time*, June 20, 1927. On May 20, 1927, in *The Spirit of St. Louis*, Lindbergh took off from Roosevelt Field, New York and landed at Le Bourget Airport, near Paris. House exaggerated the publicity received by the horned toad. Before he left, Lindbergh asked a Manhattan clipping service to save anything that might appear in print. Returning, Colonel Lindbergh learned that the bureau had filled two freight cars with clippings. He received more than 500,000 letters and 75,000 telegrams.

51 Eyewitness Bob Moore put the number of spectators at 3,000.

The pressure was lessened and a workman perforated the wall with a pick, just above the cornerstone; but, when the chain again tightened, stone and wall once more tilted forward. Again the tugging was halted and, this time, the workman nicked so deeply that when the pulling was resumed, the brick wall fell, leaving the cornerstone in place.[52]

Up to that point, House had watched everything carefully but with examination of the stone's contents imminent the stress was too great. He hurried away, hoping to avoid acquaintances who knew that his horned frog articles were responsible for the presence of the crowd. They would be quick to hold House responsible for any disappointment. He decided to view the rest of the proceedings from an office overlooking the square. Before he could reach that vantage point, crowd noises suggested that the interior of the stone was exposed and that something had been discovered.[53]

Eastland resident Edward Cox, who witnessed the entire transaction, gave this account:[54]

A story had been circulated that a horned frog, among other things, had been deposited in the cornerstone of the courthouse at the time of its building . . . and which was being demolished in February of 1928 in preparation for the erection of the present building. The

---

52 House, *Cowtown Columnist*, 4.

53 House, *Cowtown Columnist*, 5.

54 Cox, *Eastland County*, 34-35.

writer took but little interest in the story and did not intend to be present when the cornerstone was uncovered, but had strolled to the Courthouse Square and seeing the gathering went over to the location where he met Judge Cyrus B. Frost. There was a stack of window frames near the cornerstone and Mr. Frost and I climbed on them and secured a very fine view of the situation and procedure.

The cornerstone was still covered with the undisturbed section of the brick wall to a depth of three or four feet in a pyramidal shape. A tractor was near and a large chain was placed around the column and attached to the tractor. At a word from someone the tractor was put in motion and the remnant of the wall was pulled down. Men who were waiting with various tools went to the cornerstone and under the supervision of Rev. F. E. Singleton, cleared the debris away. First to be removed from direct contact with the walls of the cavity in the cornerstone was a piece of galvanized iron which snugly fitted the top of the cavity and under which were some newspapers and other articles. I then saw one of the party reach down and bring to sight a horned frog which, seemingly, was dormant, but after a few moments showed signs of life.

A man sitting on the ground between the cornerstone and Mr. Frost and myself got up, brushed his pants with his hand and as he passed remarked, "Well I'll be damned. If I had not seen it I would not believe it." That was about how the writer felt about it.

To bolster credibility, clergymen had been invited to participate in the opening that February morning.[55] As a

---

55 Church of Christ minister H. W. Wrye and H. M. Bell, pastor of the Church of God, were among those present. Ghormley, *Eastland County*, 167-168.

workman raised the plate covering the receptacle, Methodist minister Frank Singleton, who had shed his coat and rolled up his sleeves despite the cold — perhaps to show that he was concealing nothing — announced, "There's the frog!"

Oilman Eugene Day reached into the hole, picked up a dusty—and apparently dead—toad, and handed it to Singleton. Then County Judge Ed Pritchard, holding it by a hind leg, raised the frog over his head. As the crowd cheered, the lizard stirred.

While climbing the stairs, House overheard Harry H. Johnson exclaim, "They've found the frog! And the durn thing's alive."[56]

A Bible and a scrap of paper upon which Ernest Wood had written the names of his sons were found in the receptacle with the toad. (Columnist Arthur Brisbane repeated Will Wood's speculation that Rip might have drawn inspiration, stamina, and endurance from the Bible.) Blair Cherry of Ranger High School—who would become the head football coach of the University of Texas Longhorns—was photographed holding the frog.

Almost immediately the toad was given an appropriate name—Rip Van Winkle—for he had napped half again

---

56 An Army major general during World War II, Johnson would command the city of Rome. House, *Cowtown Columnist*, 4.

as long as Washington Irving's sleeping Dutchman. But had he really? Could a lizard live in darkness, without food, water, and air for a third of a century? Many questioned the toad's performance, but the doubters did not include Boyce House, who—marveling over Rip's feat—recalled some significant events of the period,

> The Maine had been sunk; the Rough Riders had dashed up San Juan Hill; Dewey had captured Manila; Bryan had been defeated two more times—and Old Rip slumbered on.
>
> A war was fought to make the world safe for democracy; oil was struck at nearby Ranger and the county was engulfed in the biggest boom earth had ever seen—but not the faintest echo reached the frog. Drouths, floods, Merkle failing to touch second base, movies, prohibition, jazz, automobiles, radio crooners—but Old Rip just kept on sleeping.[57]

The controversy over Rip's survival has never been resolved. Most Eastland residents relied upon the statements of eyewitnesses, friends who swore that no one could have tampered with the contents of the hollow stone; however, some always considered Rip's alleged longevity a hoax.

From all over the country came requests to put Rip on exhibition, while

---

57 House, *Cowtown Columnist*, 6.

The crowds continue to pour into the city to view the noted toad and enterprising photographers are reaping much money from postal cards bearing Rip's picture. Meanwhile the frog sits in a display window blinking at the queer faces of some of the thousands who peer in at him. He appears to be in no hurry to break his fast of 31 years and to date has not eaten any food although tempting morsels of bugs, worms and grass have been placed before him.

Will Wood—the owner of the lizard his father carried to the courthouse square long ago—reported that the pet was "as thin as a match" when taken from the stone, and that,

It was five or six weeks before he took anything to eat and equally as long before he could move himself along on his legs. An x-ray showed a leg broken and a few other minor injuries, but outside of that he was all right.

Two days after his release from the stone, Rip took up residence in an Eastland store window.

As yet it has not taken food and its mouth is said to have grown together. However, it is crawling about the display window with ever increasing animation. Large sums are said to have been offered for its possession."[58]

At Coleman, Sid Sackett had misgivings about the effect of the Eastland toad's fame. As the state's—perhaps

---

58 *Dallas Times Herald,* February 21, 1928.

the nation's—only horned frog breeder, he feared ruinous competition. Men in pursuit of instant wealth would destroy his monopoly by marketing toads to fill cornerstones and cages in Eastern zoos. Sackett had raised toads since 1912, when a company that sold "metalized" horned frogs ordered 200 of the lizards from him. After purchasing them from small boys for a nickel apiece and selling for a quarter, Sackett was encouraged to breed the frogs for market. Now he dreaded the commencement of another Eastland County boom—not in oil, but in horny toads.[59]

---

59 *Brownwood Bulletin*, March 12, 1928.

The Eastland County courthouse today. In the right foreground is the cornerstone from the old courthouse in which Old Rip was found. Below the window in the background is a pedestal bearing Rip's name, and inside the glass case rests the last mortal remains of the toad or one of his successors.

— Mrs. Will Wood

Old Rip at the peak of his fame. After his death he was embalmed at the Hamner Funeral Home. For years before it was put on display in the Eastland County courthouse, his body was kept in a drawer at the Abilene home of Will Wood.

— Ann Huey Bishop

The high point of Rip's tour was a meeting with President Calvin Coolidge.

Old Rip, Confidant Of Presidents

On the day following Eastland's grand opening, a Dallas newspaper proclaimed that the horned frog had been greeted by an enthusiastic throng. According to the story,

> When first taken from its score-and-a-half tomb, where no light, air, nor water had a chance to penetrate, the frog's eyes were closed and it seemed dead. Soon, however, its pale eyelids blinked and then opened. Firmly held by Eugene Day, it struggled a bit, then settled back into lethargy, seemingly ready to go to sleep for another third of a century.[60]

Spectators crowded the men who inspected the stone. Some pushed forward suddenly, posing a threat to the reptile's safety.

> County officers took charge of the frog and it will be cared for in luxury as long as it lives—or as long as they live, for they believe it will live longer than any of those who saw it resurrected. Except that its mouth seemed to have grown together, the frog was as chipper for a time as if it had awakened only from a short nap. In addition to the frog some old Eastland County newspapers, a few

---

60 *Dallas Times Herald*, February 19, 1928.

coins, and Masonic emblems were taken from the cornerstone.

The toad's diet presented an urgent problem. Red ants, its principal food, were not available at that season and attempts to feed him added to the drama. By February 22, Rip Van Winkle still had not broken his fast, but he was becoming more active and his name was soon shortened to Old Rip.[61]

> In the glass bowl in which it is kept, the frog daily shows increasing animation, tries to climb from its retainer, and even appears to be gaining in weight, but as yet, has refused to eat or drink, leading spectators to believe its mouth is sealed. Yesterday, as a feature of a day in which it drew attention from hundreds of persons, including newspaper men and photographers, the frog was inspected by Dr. Will Winton, head of the Texas Christian University biology department, and twenty teachers, assistants and students. They examined its skin and mouth and made scientific observations.[62]

Substantial amounts were offered to Wood for the privilege of showing the frog in zoos, museums, and vaudeville theaters. Curious Texans thronging Eastland bought thousands of Old Rip post cards. From a drugstore

---

61 Failing to understand the allusion to Washington Irving's story, some spelled the toad's name R. I. P.—as in "rest in peace." The nation's other major hero, Charles Lindbergh, was again flying his old Chicago-to-St. Louis mail route. After a year's absence, on Monday, February 20, he made the 286-mile trip in two hours and 53 minutes. At Chicago, six hundred well-wishers were disappointed as "Lucky Lindy" landed and drove away in a truck before fans knew of his presence.

62 *Dallas Morning News*, February 23, 1928.

window, the toad stared at the visitors while ignoring proffered bugs and worms.

Responding to some of the propositions, Will Wood took Rip on tour. On February 24, he and N. N. Day stopped in Dallas on his way to appearances in the East. The former director of the New York Zoological Gardens, Dr. William T. Hornaday, had extended an invitation for the toad to be examined by leading scientists.[63] Rip traveled in a bowl filled partially with sand.

On the day Rip went on exhibit in Dallas, the Eastland mercantile community was reminded of his value by visitors who found that Rip was gone. They complained bitterly and civic leaders were upset. Happy tourists spend money, but those travelers had expected to see the absentee frog. Travel was time-consuming and expensive, and Eastland offered very little—other than Rip—to entertain tourists. Businessmen began to question Wood's right to take the lizard out of town.[64] A reporter imagined the situation in this fashion:

> "What," the crowds exclaimed, "no frog? What sort of town is this anyhow?" And with much humph and many haws they returned, not without disappointment, to their various homes. Public-spirited Eastlanders

63 *Fort Worth Record*, February 24, 1928. Wood's father had taken the toad to the courthouse festivities. Day was the son of Eugene Day, who—after thirty-one years—extracted a live toad from the stone.

64 *Dallas Morning News*, February 27, 1928.

sprang to their city's defense. Apparently their argument brought a flush of shame to the cheeks of Wood, who had given the frog for deposit in the stone, and had received him as a prodigal when he was taken from it. All his life Wood had lived in Eastland and Eastland now was calling him—and calling for Rip.

Wood's plans to spend several days in Dallas were changed after a telephone caller mentioned litigation. An observer wrote,

Will M. Wood, the frog's custodian, was in telephonic communication with Eastland Saturday when he learned that a suit to enjoin him from showing the frog would be instituted. The fame of the frog, Mr. Wood said, had brought crowds of the curious to Eastland, who were disappointed when, seeking Eastland's frog, they learned that Rip was in Dallas. A group of Eastland citizens, probably backed by the Chamber of Commerce, said Mr. Wood, were now anxious to have the frog brought back to Eastland, claiming that Rip is now the property of the county, since the seven-year limitation statute had already applied.[65]

Wood's cancellation of the toad's scheduled appearances created new complications:

Rip is under contract to appear in Dallas, and now faces a suit for nonfulfillment. A dispute may also arise between Wood, who believes the frog is his, and the

---

65 *Dallas Morning News*, February 26, 1928.

county, which claims the frog is theirs by virtue of his having lived as their guest these thirty-one years.[66]

The exact nature of Eastland County's claim was not clear. Perhaps the commissioners were asserting a landlord's lien, since the free-loading reptile had occupied public premises for a third of a century without paying rent.[67]

While a qualified property interest can be acquired in wild creatures—animals *ferae naturae*—the right depends upon possession.[68] Young Will Wood might have been the rightful owner, but did relinquishment of possession to his father terminate his title to the toad? Did the child Will Wood voluntarily surrender custody on the day the horned frog was sealed in the stone? (Can a four-year-old legally transfer title to a parent? If not, was the taking by the father a conversion? Or was Ernest Wood the son's agent?) And could the county acquire title through the

---

66 *Dallas Morning News*, February 27, 1928. On the day Rip returned to Eastland, the City of Dallas was deciding what improvements would be required if it purchased Love Field from the Army Air Corps.

67 H. A. McCanlies stated, "I later learned that some three separate claimants claimed the ownership of the frog. One was the contractor as part of the salvage, one by the county in dispute of salvage claims, and one by Mr. Wood who placed the frog in the stone. All claims were finally settled by placing the frog in the courthouse lobby in a casket manufactured especially for the frog by the American Casket Company and donated to the county."

68 William T. Fryer, *Readings on Personal Property*, St. Paul: West Publishing Company, 1938, 57-58. Professor Fryer, of Texas extraction, dealt with the law of animals *ferae naturae* in the initial week of his Property II course at the George Washington University Law School; forty years later, this is my first chance to make use of that knowledge.

father if the pet was wrongfully taken from the child? Those questions might have been considered, but probably were not. The truth was that Eastland County's commissioners had not given much thought to the equities; they simply *wanted* the frog kept available for the entertainment and edification of potential customers of Eastland storekeepers.[69]

The horny toad was back in Dallas on March 10, when both Woods—father and son—were sued for breach of contract and $6,296.25 in damages. Dick Perry, of Dallas, claimed that he was to exhibit the frog for half the paid admissions, but the Woods had refused to perform. By virtue of a writ of attachment, a constable seized the lizard and forbade its removal from Dallas County pending trial of Perry's suit.[70]

When Will Wood warned that the reptile was worth $50,000 and that the county and constable would be liable should Rip suffer harm, anxious Dallas businessmen decided the frog and the controversy should be gotten out of town. Rip might well die in custody. After all, the fragile creature had endured three decades of solitary confinement already. The frog was probably living on borrowed time and

---

69 The county dads may have assumed that Rip was part of Eastland County's flora and fauna and belonged to the citizenry, for whom the county commissioners were fiduciaries.

70 *Brownwood Bulletin*, March 10, 1928.

a premature death would be embarrassing and would precipitate expensive litigation. Former mayor William L. Holland posted a $1,000 bond to release the attachment. Carrying the celebrated toad in a brown paper sack, the secretary of Eastland's Chamber of Commerce scurried out of Dallas before more legal problems could develop.[71]

Another New York trip was scheduled. The motorcade would follow the route promoters were calling "The Broadway of America."[72] The Dallas legal skirmishing had caused some delay, which may have whetted the natural curiosity of Texans and increased the numbers hoping to see Rip. He attracted huge crowds in Royce City and Greenville, and 10,000 enthusiastic Hopkins Countians welcomed the frog to Sulphur Springs.

Doubts of the legitimacy of the Rip story did not reduce attendance at the St. Louis Zoological Society's reptile house, where, on April 29, the toad was greeted by 40,000 Missourians.

So many people came to see him yesterday that special guards were called to dissolve the blockades.

---

71 *New York Times*, May 6, 1928. Another Dallas ambition concerned moving Baylor University from Waco. An education commission had suggested relocating the university from the town of 60,000 to the city of 300,000. The Dallas Chamber of Commerce offered $1.5 million to Baylor and citizens' groups pledged a thousand-acre campus. The commission's vote to accept the Dallas proposition would affect the future of thirteen-year-old Southern Methodist University.

72 The Broadway of America route began in Los Angeles and ended in New York City. Later it was Highway 80.

Attendants at the reptile house had expected unusual crowds, but not for St. Louis to come out in a body to see Old Rip. Some persons jeered at the placard over the glass case in which the toad was exhibited which set forth that Rip lived 31 years without air or water or food. But scoffers and believers alike came to see the small reptile which seemed not at all perturbed by the thousands of eyes that peered at him.

The St. Louis Zoo—which had paid Wood to exhibit Rip—offered $1,000 to anyone who could disprove the toad's claimed history. A newspaper reporter stated, "Some of the spectators, eager to earn the $1,000, asked Rip about himself, but he merely blinked at the too personal questions and continued to search his cage for ants." The crowd—said to be the largest ever to visit an animal exhibit in St. Louis—became unruly when attendants tried to shut down the premises at closing time. Wood found it necessary to deny a rumor that he had sold the toad to the St. Louis Zoo.

From Wheeling, West Virginia, Rip and company headed for Washington, where at 12:30 p. m. on May 3, the renowned toad enjoyed a fifteen-minute audience with President Calvin Coolidge.[73] A reporter stated that

---

73 *New York Times*, May 4, 1928. *Dallas Morning News*, February 25, 1928. An earlier visit by Texas Indian chiefs, may have facilitated this presidential interview. On February 24, Chief Sunkee, of the Alabama tribe, and his aide, McConnico Battise, were in Washington to testify for a bill providing land and tools for the Alabama in Polk County, Texas. President Coolidge hosted them at the White House.

Although the President's day was completely filled, he made a place to receive the Texas visitor when Senator Earle B. Mayfield told the White House that he wanted to exhibit the famous Texas reptile.[74] About 300 visitors to shake hands with the President waited in the outer offices while the toad escorted by the Texas visitors were with the president. . . . Mr. Coolidge examined the toad carefully and viewed as remarkable that the reptile had such reputed life power.

When Wood attempted to introduce himself, the president quickly interrupted, saying, "Yes, Yes, let me see the horned frog."[75] The *New York Times* reported that

President Coolidge today met one of the world's famous toads—"Old Rip," who for thirty-one years is reputed to have been entombed in the cornerstone of the Eastland, Texas, Court House. Old Rip spent more than fifteen minutes on the Chief Executive's mahogany desk, having been brought to the White House by its owner, Will M. Wood. Mr. Coolidge peered into the gold fish bowl that is now the horned creature's home. He played safe by using his horn-rimmed spectacles as

---

74 *New York Times*, May 3, 1928. On the previous day, Coolidge welcomed the German-Irish crew of the Junkers monoplane *Bremen*—Baron Gunther von Huenefeld, Captain Hermann Koehl, and Major James Fitzmaurice—who were given the Distinguished Flying Cross for making the first non-stop westward crossing of the North Atlantic. The three airmen received a state welcome, which included a tribute at the tomb of the Unknown Soldier. Among the participants were Secretary of State Frank Kellogg, Colonel Charles Lindbergh, and Captain Edward V. Rickenbacker—the leading American ace of World War I.

75 *Dallas Morning News*, January 18, 1964.

a pointer to indicate the numerous ridges on Old Rip's head and back.[76]

Coolidge stroked the frog's back with his spectacles, and "the President and Old Rip gazed steadily at each other for a full minute without a sound—Silent Cal had met his match."[77] Wood reported to the people of Eastland by telegram that

> The president's remarks to Rip were not announced to the public but are assumed to have been friendly rather than scientific. It is stated that Rip blinked his pleasure at meeting the president but did not enter into any extended conversation.

After White House correspondents photographed the horny toad, Wood left for New York to submit the lizard for inspection by skeptical scientists and believers such as Dr. Hornaday, a leading expert on animal and reptile life.[78] Rip was the star of a movie that Wood narrated. Since red ants were not available in Manhattan, "a professional bug

---

76 *New York Times,* May 6, 1928. Governor Al Smith was the leading candidate for the Democratic presidential nomination, and Herbert Hoover was the favorite of the Republicans. Responding to a Supreme Court decision that would have exempted the president from the income tax, the Senate passed a bill subjecting presidential income to taxation. The governor of Rome, in New York City, proclaimed that Mussolini was a "man of destiny."

77 House, *Cowtown Columnist,* 10.

78 *Dallas Morning News,* May 4, 1928. Interesting newspaper features included "Tales of Real Dogs," by Albert Payson Terhune, in the *News,* and "Favorite Jokes of Famous People" in the *Dallas Times Herald.*

catcher provided a suitable substitute, at fifty cents per bug, and the cameras showed Rip feasting."[79]

Rip's publicity may have prompted some Californians to stage a contest inspired by Mark Twain's jumping frog story.[80] More horny toad litigation occurred in Eastland County that summer, although Rip was not involved. President I. G. Jones, of the Dallas Lions Club, asked his brother-in-law, G. T. Rheubotham, to help buy some toads in Ranger. Rheubotham persuaded a reporter to write a story about Jones' intention to pay a dime apiece for horned frogs. On the scheduled day, Jones' son was greeted by young Ranger entrepreneurs hawking their wares—thousands of the lizards. The oversupply knocked the bottom out of the local market. While they were paid a dime for some of the lizards, sellers received a nickel for others. Before he stopped buying, Jones was paying only 2 1/2 cents each and some unhappy dealers were left with their inventories intact.

Young Doyce Shelby complained that his 234 toads had brought just over $11—only 4.7 cents apiece. His father, W. S. Shelby, filed suit for $197.25 in an Eastland

---

79 House, *Cowtown Columnist*, 9.

80 *New York Times*, May 6, 1928. Promoters of the "Jumping Frog Jubilee" at Angels Camp, California announced that the event would be held on May 19, that the barroom floor in the old hotel was being cleaned, and searchers were catching contestants for the main event commemorating Mark Twain's "Jumping Frog of Calveras County."

justice of the peace court and obtained a writ of attachment on the Jones truck and the 1,200 frogs young Jones had purchased. Dr. Jones hurried to Ranger to post a $400 replevin bond to release his son's truck and cargo.

A group photograph was made to commemorate the litigation. Justice of the Peace J. N. McFatter, the younger Jones, and the constable who made the levy, posed with a dozen witnesses—boys and girls—who were left with a thousand unsold frogs after Jones stopped buying. The extraordinary photo appeared in newspapers the next day.[81]

Rip's New York trip lasted about six weeks. Afterward he resumed his role as pet at Will Wood's home.[82] The horned frog was sought out by visitors, who — no doubt — imposed upon the hospitality of the family. Edith Wood Grissom, a daughter of Will Wood, wrote:

> Old Rip was my pet. He dashed from an ant bed in front of a truck with me in pursuit, and later to a vacant lot where I had released 250 horned frogs. He was easy to find as he was gray with worn horns and a limp from a broken leg. He hibernated in a goldfish bowl, so I put him on the back porch. He froze! [83]

---

81 *Dallas Morning News*, July 1, 1928. Seldom do the plaintiff, defendant, judge, constable, and a score of horny toad entrepreneurs sit for a photograph.

82 Mrs. Will Wood, interview, September 29, 1979.

83 *The History of Eastland County, Texas*, 599.

The frog's worn — or missing — horns were cited as evidence that he had spent decades in the cornerstone. Proponents pointed out that the typical horned toad sheds its horns during hibernation and grows new ones in the period after the sleep. Never having had that opportunity, Rip did not replace his horns.[84] Another theory urged by critics of Ernest Wood's experiment, was that the frog had worn away his horns on the stone's interior walls while he was a frustrated, unhappy prisoner trying to escape.

Rip died of pneumonia on January 19, 1929, after a norther struck Eastland. The announcement of the sad event read,

> The body was found late Saturday. Rip's head was protruding above the leaves and sand in which he had been hibernating since his asserted emergence from the stone witnessed by pastors and other leading citizens, some of whom signed affidavits to the genuineness of the veteran's removal. While there was no inquest, the popular verdict was that Rip, lured out by the sunshine, was chilled fatally. Details concerning the disposition of the body have not been announced.[85]

84 House, *Cowtown Columnist*, 8.

85 *Dallas Morning News*, January 20, 1929. Rip's obituary was flanked by stories on the impeachment of Oklahoma governor Henry S. Johnston, the signing of the Kellogg Peace Treaty, and the opposition of some Dallas pastors to an anti-evolution bill pending in the Texas House of Representatives.

A judge granted Wood's request to have Rip embalmed. Attendants at the Barrow Undertaking Company used special instruments to accomplish the task, and Rip was laid out in a tiny, satin-lined coffin donated by the National Casket Company.

The Will Woods family moved to Abilene in 1936. Rip's body remained in their home until after World War II, when they turned it over to Eastland County for display in a handsome marble and glass mausoleum in the courthouse lobby. Because of a security problem—pranksters kept stealing the dead toad—in the early seventies a viewing window was installed in the front wall of the courthouse. Protected from meddlers by two layers of glass, Rip's remains are visible from inside and outside the courthouse so the curious and the believers can pay their respects at any hour of the day or night. It is Eastland County's equivalent of the Vladimir Ilich Lenin tomb in Moscow.[86]

Much of civic life in Eastland has been influenced by Old Rip's history and legend. Businesses have proudly worn his name. Curious motorists stopped in Eastland because of the legendary frog and when Highway 80 bordered the square, Eastland had more filling stations per capita than any other Texas city. Five thousand vehicles

---

86 In 1969, when Larry Nance and I were putting together *The Texas Courthouse*, the coffin was on display in the lobby, but in June of 1975 I discovered that the courthouse had been remodeled and the show window in the front wall installed.

passed through town daily and horny toads were given as premiums with the purchase of gasoline. While most citizens considered the Old Rip tradition good for the community, some protested a connection they deemed limiting and embarrassing.

Rip's mortal remains have suffered since his death. City fathers were accustomed to showing the dessicated lizard to honored visitors, and a certain amount of wear and tear was inevitable. A persistent myth concerned John Connally's 1962 visit during his first campaign for governor. Eastland Democrats planned to donate the dead toad to Connally. A Chamber of Commerce representative would hand Rip (in his coffin) to the candidate as they stood on the back platform of his special train. The Eastlanders would then ride with Connally to Cisco, where Rip would be recovered and brought home. The hope was that Eastland would derive much valuable publicity from the theatrics. Unfortunately, photographers asked the candidate to pose with Rip and Connally picked him up by a leg. The Democrats' worst fears were realized, for—legend had it— a fragile limb broke off. Some declared that Connally's carelessness and the resulting damage to Eastland's most important personage kept him from carrying the county.

Actually, the Connally story was pure rumor, perhaps politically motivated. The leg had been lost years before when the toad's remains were kept in Will Wood's home. Daughter Jan Wood was showing the frog to a young friend, who removed Rip from the casket and accidentally tore off the brittle leg.[87]

In 1949, Eastland held its first horny toad celebration. Boyce House presided and the main event was the Old Rip Horned Toad Derby, a race in which competing toads were placed in a ring and the fleetest—the first out of the circle—won $100 for the owner or sponsor. Participants from throughout the nation each paid $5 to enter a frog.

In the 1950 derby the 435 steeds included Edgar Bergen's entry, Mortimer Snerd, which won a heat but lost the sweepstakes to Lonely Hart, carrying the colors of Fort Worth's Marion Hart. Among 500 entries in the following year were Bergen's Mortimer Snerd, II and a speedy reptile sponsored by Chrysler Corporation president L. L. Colbert.[88] The 1951 Horned Toad Derby Queen reigned over a street square dance.[89] For years the event was not held, but in

---

87 Mrs. Will Wood, interview, September 29, 1979.

88 After a student asked about Mortimer Snerd, I realized that few young people have heard of Edgar Bergen and Charlie McCarthy—much less Mortimer Snerd. Long ago, in those better times, ventriloquist Edgar Bergen, his red-headed dummy Charlie McCarthy, and country cousin Mortimer Snerd entertained American families on network radio each Sunday evening. In present terms, Edgar Bergen was the father of actress Candice Bergen, who is Murphy Brown on television.

89 *Dallas Morning News*, July 22, 1951.

1964 Mayor Don Pierson announced that the city was considering its revival.[90]

In 1967, Eastland entered a horned frog in the thirty-first annual Coalinga, California "Toad Gallop." No contestant was native to the area; all came from Texas, Arizona, and New Mexico. Evidently, insecticides had wiped out Coalinga's resident horned frogs. A contestant paid a $10 application fee to the Coalinga Chamber of Commerce and was assigned a toad if he did not furnish one.[91]

Rip's legend is such an integral part of Eastland's image that mention of the city usually brings up the cornerstone story. In 1964, the Eastland city council was considering an ordinance forbidding the sale and use of cigarettes. Inquiries came from throughout the country. The "pestiferous" telephone calls Mayor Pierson received in the middle of the night from "all over the hemisphere" helped the governing body to abandon the ordinance. The mayor said, "Some of these people must have been at parties when they called me, judging by the late hours when the phone would ring." Reporters padded their accounts of the anti-smoking effort with summaries of the Rip tale. The tobacco ordinance provided an excuse for newspapers to inform a new generation about Old Rip.

---

90 *Dallas Morning News*, January 18, 1964.

91 *Dallas Morning News*, April 10, 1967.

Through the years numerous Eastland promotions included the staged kidnapping and recovery of Rip's mortal remains. (The frognapper would retain the body until some charitable goal—in, for instance, a blood drive or fundraiser—was attained.) Close observers noted that Rip did not always look like himself after his rescue. Sometimes he had grown a new leg or he came back with the wrong limb missing. (In a time when horned frogs were plentiful, some of those charged with recovering Rip from the malefactor realized the practical solution was to simply go outside and pick up a substitute. Few citizens knew Rip by appearance.) Some critics alleged that imposters were regularly introduced after frognappings and claimed that the original Rip was lost long ago.

On January 16, 1973 Rip—or whatever horny toad occupied the casket—was stolen from the courthouse. The substitution of an imposter provoked the kidnapper to write a letter that James Dabney quoted in an Abilene newspaper:

> To the public. The purpose of this writing is to clarify the mystery surrounding the disappearance of Old Rip. . . . I am the person who removed Old Rip from public display and he definitely remains in my posses-sion as the enclosed photograph should establish beyond any doubt. . . . I had planned to remain silent but this attempt to keep "the legend of Old Rip" alive by

replacing him with an obvious fake has forced me to tell my story.[92]

I am one of three surviving perpetrators of the hoax which grew into "the legend of Old Rip." One evening some 45 years ago five young men, including myself, decided to place a live horned frog in the cornerstone in the old courthouse which had just been demolished. With a little help from a member of the demolition crew we were able to lift the cornerstone and toss the horned toad inside. The cornerstone was reopened the next day at the ceremony . . . we were all surprised at the amount of excitement caused by our prank . . . . However, in recent years I have become increasingly regretful of our actions so long ago. I have seen various community leaders and organizations eagerly exploiting Old Rip and neglecting many civic responsibilities which are so vital to a small town today.[93]

Attempting to prevent Eastland from "building its future around a dried-up horned frog," the writer had stolen Old Rip; however,

Several days later I was dismayed to learn that a new Old Rip had appeared in the courthouse. I proceeded to remove this rather poor imitation and the coffin lay empty for almost a year. Nevertheless another fake was produced last week during the livestock show. I then realized it was useless to continue abducting all the imposter Old Rips and the only way to end it was by telling the truth once and for all.

92 *Abilene Reporter-News*, March 30, 1974.

93 *Abilene Reporter-News*, March 30, 1974.

Finally accepting defeat, the kidnapper promised to return the authentic toad by mail upon removal of the most recent pretender. The remains on display in Eastland may or may not be the body of the original Rip, the truth is known to Him only who marks the fall of the sparrow.

A Debate On
Horned Frog Longevity

Controversy over the life span and vitality of horny frogs existed long before the Eastland cornerstone was invaded; but on Saturday, February 18, 1928, with the removal of Old Rip, the argument was sharpened and intensified, as new participants entered the lists. Debate has continued through the years by the informed, the somewhat informed, and the holders of opinions. There is no proof that any minds have been changed by evidence or advocacy.

Bill Kittrell—who was in Eastland when the imprisoned horned lizard awoke to find himself a celebrity—advised, in a time when Texans probably believed more passionately than now in their special place in the universe,

> Write stories that George Washington was a congenital liar. Write stories in favor of sin. But don't write any expose that Old Rip was a phoney.[94]

---

94 *Dallas Morning News*, January 18, 1964. Years ago, I was a secretary to Senator Lyndon Baines Johnson; on November 1, 1950, Dallas public relations man Bill Kittrell rushed into the office to report that several men had tried to kill the president. Harry Truman was living in the Blair House temporarily while repairs were made to the White House. The assassins killed Capitol Police officer Leslie Coffelt at his post in front of Blair House.

Realizing how preposterous the frog story might seem to those who were not present at Rip's debut, eyewitnesses rushed to the defense. Eastland founder Charles U. Connellee, who had watched Eugene Day free the lizard from the stone, warned that regional prejudices would be a factor in the skepticism shown the Eastland story.

> Every loyal Texan inherently knows that a Texas horned toad will live for 100 years without food or air if he remains in Texas. It's just jealousy of Texas that is causing these scientific doubts about that toad.[95]

The only fact upon which everyone agreed was that a live toad was removed from the stone in Eastland on that winter day in 1928. The question was then: How long had Rip been an unwilling tenant of the county—a third of a century, or only a few hours?

Merchant M. W. McMinn, of Olden, Eastland County, told an Associated Press representative that in 1897 he saw Sandy Martin deposit the frog, three newspapers, a Bible, and other articles inside the cornerstone. On the next day, worried that someone might have meddled with the lizard, McMinn lifted the cover and found the toad alive and well.[96]

---

95 He was living in Oklahoma City when he made this statement. *Dallas Morning News*, February 22, 1928.

96 House, *Cowtown Columnist,* 11.

McMinn was contradicted by S. P. Willard, of Denison, who stated—a few days after the 1928 opening—that no horned frog was left in the cornerstone in 1897. Willard explained that,

> During the ceremony the stone was held about eight feet in the air by a derrick. After it was set in position Captain June Kimbell placed a copy of the *Eastland Chronicle* published that week and Rev. B. F. Chastain, then county judge, laid a small Bible in the stone before it was sealed. Also several coins and business cards were placed in the stone and that was all.[97]

Another eyewitness, Tulsa barber W. H. Day—a laborer who helped build the new Eastland temple of justice—stated that there was no toad inside the cornerstone until a few hours before the February 1928 opening, when he, his brother Eugene Day, contractor John White, and superintendent Henry Cobb dropped the future Rip into the cavity. Day said, "There was a horned toad there and it was suggested we put it in the cornerstone. This we did."[98]

Affirming that he helped extricate a live horny toad from the ruined Eastland courthouse, the Reverend F. E. Singleton stated that he had been ordered to insure that nothing shady occurred at the opening.

---

97 *Dallas Morning News*, February 22, 1928.
98 *Dallas Morning News*, February 21, 1928. Day did not explain how a horny toad was available during hibernation season.

I knew my business and I was not interested in anything else taken out of the cornerstone. I was watching to see if a frog really was in there and that none other was substituted. When some of the articles were removed, I looked down into the box and was the first man to see the frog. I cried out, "There's the frog." Then I asked Mr. [Eugene] Day to pick it up and hand it to me. He did. I took the frog in my hand and suddenly it wiggled its hind leg. I then cried out: "It's alive." I held it up for the crowd to see. I am positive there was no hoax perpetrated.[99]

Although some Eastland citizens suspected the contractor of committing a fraud, James Golden recalled that he and twenty others stood guard at the wrecked courthouse all night just prior to the opening "to see to it that there wasn't no hanky panky."[100]

H. A. McCanlies asserted that, on the morning of the great day, a ten-foot high brick wall rested on the cornerstone. Officer Hammett herded spectators away as Harry Wood (a son of Ernest Wood) backed his truck into position, threw a cable around the wall and—with a winch—pulled down most of the bricks. Even then, the hole in the stone was not exposed. A man pried away the rest of the bricks with a pinch bar, but mortar and a thick lead sheet still covered the cavity. McCanlies said,

99 *Dallas Morning News*, February 22, 1928.
100 Jim Golden interview at Eastland on June 3, 1975.

After the seal was removed, Bob Hammett asked the Rev. Frank E. Singleton, pastor of the First Methodist Church, to take out the contents. Although it was a cold day he removed his coat, rolled up his sleeves and took out the contents. There were old newspapers, old Bibles, coins and other things. The paper, being rotten, fell to pieces and he then lifted out the horned frog. However, he did not look like a frog, but a piece of bark off an oak tree. The Reverend held him by the tail and then after a moment his legs began to move and after a few deep breaths of air he began to fill out and looked like a frog again. He was then placed in the south sunlit window of Madden's Drugstore. After being fed some flies, small pieces of meat and different insects obtainable in the winter, he began to fill out to natural size. Inasmuch as his principal food is red ants, naturally unobtainable in the winter and this being on February 18 he seemed to thrive on other food. You will please note that inasmuch as horned frogs hibernate from early winter until the latter part of April or the middle of May it would have been impossible for anyone to have obtained the frog and placed him in the stone as claimed by some people.[101]

Superintendent H. A. Parks, of the Christy Dolph Construction Company—which had contracted to raze the courthouse—declared that the stone "had not been tampered with, and I saw the frog half-covered with dust, in the cavity. It appeared to be dead and was as flat as a dollar." Another construction worker, Roy Whatley, said,

I picked the concrete from off the top of the cornerstone with a pick and know the stone had not been

---

101 Clipping from an unidentified newspaper dated April 2, 1972.

tampered with. I also saw the frog in the stone. It appeared to be dead and was very flat. I watched it for some time after it was lifted out and saw it when it began to show signs of life.[102]

Eugene Day—who lifted the toad to freedom—added,

I saw the frog partially covered with dust in the cavity of the stone. I did not put my hand on it until I called the attention of the Rev. F. E. Singleton, standing nearby, to the fact that the frog was there. It was some time before I took hold of it.

County Judge Ed Pritchard stated,

The frog was already in the cornerstone and no one could have put it in there when the stone was opened. Neither do I see any chance or any evidence of the stone having been opened beforehand.

Some atttacks on the Old Rip story have received less attention than others because informants refused to be identified, although a reluctance to become embroiled in the controversy was understandable. In 1968, reporter Tommy Ayres quoted an unnamed Dallasite who claimed that he and two friends broke into the cornerstone and deposited the frog a week before the opening; he said that what began as a prank simply got out of hand.[103]

---

102 *Dallas Morning News,* February 21, 1928.
103 *Dallas Times Herald,* March 3, 1968.

Responding to the news from Eastland, Robert Grounds, of Dallas County, cited a similar incident. About 1900 he was quarrying limestone to build a chimney when

> Upon splitting one of the thick slabs a tiny toad about the size of one's thumb was found. It was white, or nearly so, and was alive when found, made a few convulsive movements and died. How long this little reptile had been entombed in that ledge of limestone is unknown. It had probably been there for centuries. How it got there is also problematical. Perhaps it became imprisoned when the material of the rock was in a plastic state. . . . The pyramids may be younger than was the little toad.[104]

Another horny toad was discovered by Mrs. Charles M. Kessler in Austin. In 1883, when blasting for the new capitol's foundation disturbed her sick husband, Mrs. Kessler asked the foreman to refrain from using explosives for the rest of the day.[105] She said,

> He agreed, and I walked about a bit over the ground, for I am a student of geology. At one spot where the charges had torn loose the limestone I noticed three round grayish brown stones. My attention was called to them because they had been embedded in the limestone and were smooth, apparently having been water-washed.

---

104 *Dallas Morning News*, February 22, 1928.

105 *Dallas Morning News*, February 1928. The excavation was commenced in 1882. Senator Temple Houston made the dedication speech for the new capitol in May 1888.

I picked up one about ten inches in diameter and struck it against a protruding piece of limestone. The rock cracked in half like a walnut and to my amazement in the center I found a flattened toad frog. When it was freed from its rock home it puffed up large and took several hops. The frog lived about fifteen minutes. I cracked both of the other rocks, but found no frogs in them.[106]

The frog had probably been in the rock for ages, I was told by a geologist at the time. The half pieces of stone, one showing an impression of the frog, were taken to the museum in the old capitol building. I don't know whether or not they are there now. I was told that the frog would be preserved.

Soon after the Eastland incident, workmen removing a fifteen-year-old wall in San Antonio's Gunter Hotel uncovered a toad that could not open its jaws, had only three legs, and was "as flat as a pancake and covered with a hard crust of mortar." To revive the lizard, hotel employees soaked it in water.[107]

In support of Rip's authenticity, Abilene banker J. V. Howerton told of an East Texas occurrence:

Forty years ago, in Nacogdoches County while I was digging a well I dug up at a depth of thirty-five feet a live toad which was in a perfectly air-tight tomb of dirt,

---

106 *Dallas Morning News*, February 22, 1928.
107 *Dallas Morning News*, July 14, 1928.

gravel, and clay. We had to break the ball with a pick after we discovered one of the frog's legs sticking out. He was perfectly flat when found, but soon puffed himself up and hopped off, as chipper as you please. There are a good many things these smart aleck scientists don't know.[108]

Mrs. George K. Wassell imagined a great age for an imprisoned toad she saw in Dallas:

In 1906 several members of my family and two Eastern college professors went out to White Rock Creek, where the professors were interested in studying some rock formations. Some of us began throwing rocks into the creek. One of the professors picked up a large rock weighing about forty or fifty pounds and hurled it against another boulder to break it. From almost the exact center we found a flat, almost colorless frog which was alive. The imprint of the frog in the rock showed that he had become embedded in it while the rock was yet soft perhaps ages ago. We left the frog there, but went back after it the next day and found that it had evidently gained strength to hop away. We could not find it.[109]

In 1930, Curator J. B. Thoburn, of the Oklahoma State Historical Society, found three live toads in a Beaver County Indian mound.[110] Thoburn estimated the age of the lizards at three or four centuries. At first, their eyes and

---

108 *Dallas Morning News*, February 22, 1928.
109 *Dallas Morning News*, February 22, 1928.
110 The mound was believed to have been part of an ancient pueblo.

mouths were sealed, but within moments they hopped about and could see. A Museum of National History employee journeyed to Frederick, Oklahoma to inspect the reptiles and the site. He declared that "an animal doesn't live forever or even half of forever."[111]

Stimulated by the Eastland story, R. B. Moore, of Zephyr—in neighboring Brown County—wrote that

> I moved to Callahan County in 1897 and settled on a piece of vacant land about 1 1/2 miles north of Glen Cove. I built a log cabin to live in and in getting out rock for a chimney I dug up a rock about the size of a man's head. I burst the rock open and out jumped a toad frog. Of course, I don't know how long the frog had been housed in the rock but from the size of the rock it must have been over a hundred years. Of course, I have no way of now proving the frog was in the rock but I would be willing to take an oath to that effect.[112]

At Brownwood, Howard Payne College professor O. E. Winebrenner declared Rip's performance to be credible—under the conditions of his confinement—and cited an experience with a snake:

> On the 7th of October, 1925, one of my students brought me from the neighborhood of the Jim Ned [Creek] a very large and very fine specimen of the Texas

---

111 *Austin American-Statesman*, September 30, 1930.

112 *Brownwood Bulletin*, March 2, 1928.

Rattler. For a number of months I housed this rattler in a plate glass aquarium through which a tiny stream of water was kept running. After about six months this rattler was transferred to a so-called hood or glass cabinet in my Chemistry laboratory. This reptile remained in this case until the 14th of June 1927, when he died. During the twenty and more months of his captivity he never swallowed a bit of food. Water, however, was always available.[113]

I was informed by those who captured this rattler that he had been without food some two weeks when he was brought to my laboratory. My report is that he lived six hundred and twenty-two days without any food. He did have plenty of water, however, and plenty of air.

Furthermore, the death of this rattler was not brought on by starvation. He had been provoked many times into striking the plate glass behind which he was housed. His mouth had been bruised and infected from his own poison. This led directly to his death. Had he not been disturbed so many times, thereby losing so much of his energy, I am of the opinion that he would have lived twice as long.

The famous Van Winkle Toad had practically ideal conditions under which to hibernate. If the story is true the explanation probably lies in this favorable environment.

Among West Texans sufficiently challenged to research the horny toad's vitality was a Brownwood editor

---

113 *Brownwood Bulletin*, March 1, 1928.

who reported that the subject of his experiment, a horned frog named George, was "taking his imprisonment in a cell in the Central Drug Store window with much composure."[114] George was well and happy but had shown no inclination to hibernate—perhaps because of excessive light in the store window—and therefore,

> George will be removed to a dark room in the *Bulletin* building after remaining on exhibition for a short time or it is possible that he will be placed in some other place for safe keeping and in surroundings which will be more nearly like those of Rip Van Winkle of Eastland.

Several scientists believed Rip's survival had been due to the moisture and air admitted through the porous stone in which he had been imprisoned. Professor Winebrenner believed the *Bulletin* should afford George similar conditions:

> Permit me to advise you that the sealed glass jar will be an unfair test. The recess in this case would be impervious to moisture, and would not permit the diffusion of gases as would the stone. Also the light admitted would play an important part in the more rapid rate of metabolism in your specimen. Neither would you be fair in confining a horned toad at this time of the year since he has already been in hibernation since last fall.

---

114 *Brownwood Bulletin*, March 2, 1928. The toad furnished by young George Barlow was named in his honor.

Professor Sam McInnis, of Brownwood's Daniel Baker College, also took the *Bulletin* to task over the experiment:

> I do not know all the facts in the Eastland story. From what I know about the story I think that it is true, because the frog was entombed in a sand rock, and it is possible for moisture and oxygen to pass through the rock and reach the frog, and sustain life for an indefinite length of time.
>
> In regard to the frog which you have sealed in an air tight container, I do not think that it will live one year, provided the glass container is air-tight. If you had placed your frog in a sand rock, sealed it, and then placed the rock out where it would be exposed to the rain I think it would be possible for your frog to live one year but in an air tight glass bottle, I don't think it possible, however, nothing is impossible with God.[115]

The *Bulletin* editor may have tired of the experiment, or his skin may not have been sufficiently thick to withstand adverse comment on George's incarceration. Whatever the motive, the newspaper's ill-conceived effort ended after thirty days.[116]

After testing several toads, Baylor University professor George E. Potter announced that an average-sized

---

115 *Brownwood Bulletin*, March 1, 1928.
116 House, *Cowtown Columnist*, 7.

horned frog could survive about two months at low temperatures while penned in a space containing a liter of air.[117]

In 1972, Dr. Albert Outler, of Southern Methodist University, a distinguished theologian, asked Frank X. Tolbert for information on Old Rip. While researching sermons of Methodist founder John Wesley, Outler found an intriguing reference to frogs. Wesley, who lived from 1703 to 1791, mentioned

> A late incident, the truth of which cannot be reasonably doubted, there having been so large a number of witnesses. An ancient oak being cut down and split through the midst, out of the very heart of the tree crept a large toad and walked away with all the speed he could. Now, how long may we imagine had this creature continued there? It is not unlikely it might have remained in its nest above 100 years. It is not improbable it was nearly if not altogether coeval with the oak; having been in some way or another enclosed therein at the time that it was planted. It had lived that strange kind of life at least a century.[118]

Outler traced Wesley's tale to a book in which Oliver Goldsmith asked,

> What shall we say to its (the toad) living for centuries lodged in the bottom of a rock or cased within the body

---

117 G. E. Potter, "Suffocation Point in the Horned Lizard, *Phrynosoma Cornutum*", *Science*, Vol. 73, 314-315.

118 *Dallas Morning News*, February 24, 1928. John Wesley's sermon was entitled "On Living Without God." Not having read it, I rely upon Tolbert and Dr. Outler.

of an oak tree without the smallest access for nourish-
ment or air, and yet taken out alive and perfect. . . . We
have the highest authorities bearing witness their truth,
and yet the whole analogy of nature seems to arraign
them of falsehood. Bacon asserts that toads are found in
this manner. . . . [119]

An early critic of the Eastland story, New York
Zoological Gardens curator Raymond L. Ditmars, asserted
that a toad might endure three or four months of confinement, but he believed their reputation for extraordinary
vitality came from lizards having been discovered alive
after rock was blasted; however, those cases were not
precedent for Old Rip in that the reptiles had only recently
crawled into fissures in the rock and had not been without
food and air.[120]

Although the University of Texas had no reptile
expert, Austin scientists were skeptical of Eastland's horned
frog tale. So was Indiana University Zoology professor D.
W. Hamlett, who had kept horned lizards without food or
water for five months. In a state of suspended animation,
Hamlett believed a toad might survive a few years—but not
thirty.

119 *Dallas Morning News*, February 24, 1928. I haven't read this one either.
Tolbert said this quotation came from the seventh volume of Oliver Goldsmith's
An History of the Earth and Animated Nature, which was published in 1774.
120 *Dallas Morning News*, February 21, 1928.

On the other hand, Austin College Biology professor Prentiss F. Reid believed a toad could survive three decades in confinement. Since the horned frog was a dormant animal, he could exist for extreme periods if the stone's interior remained sufficiently damp.[121]

An early belief in the Rip episode was manifested by Dr. William T. Hornaday, who submitted this experience:

> I was in Ceylon digging for elephant bones and tusks in sand which was packed so hard it had almost the consistency of rock. So far as could be observed that sand had been lying there for a thousand years. In this impermeable mass about two feet below the surface, we uncovered a frog which was absolutely entombed there. Fortunately it escaped spades and pickaxes and was lifted out alive. Its stomache was full of water, which it ejected and then hopped away. It opened my eyes to the possibility of things at which the scientists are prone to scoff. It was impossible for the frog to have entered the excavation after it had been dug; it was uncovered by a shovel in part of the soil which had not been touched. There was no fissure or burrows anywhere in that indurated mass.[122]

Boyce House, who brought national attention to the cornerstone opening at Eastland, did not expect the frog to be found alive, but after Rip was released he became a strong advocate of the horny toad's extraordinary vitality.

---

121 *Dallas Morning News*, February 21, 1928.
122 *Dallas Times Herald*, February 22, 1928.

House gave voice to the prevailing quandry by quoting an old farmer: "I know it happened, because I saw it; I know it didn't happen, because it just don't make sense." He argued,

> Well, there are men in the penitentiary today who were sent there on circumstantial evidence not as strong as the proof which supports Old Rip's claim. Ernest Wood told of placing a frog there. At the same time he told of this, he mentioned also that he had handed over a piece of paper bearing the names of his sons Willie (as Will was called in early boyhood) and Harry. When the cornerstone was opened, a faded piece of paper bearing the names of the Wood brothers was found.
>
> We have seen, therefore, that a frog was placed in the cornerstone and we have seen that one was removed almost thirty-one years later—and recall the circumstances of the removal; the cornerstone so firmly attached to the wall above that they almost toppled over together when the truck chain tugged; and the hundreds of pairs of eyes gazing intently as the stone was opened. . . . This audience was above, below, all around; and it was in the clear light of day.[123]

---

123 House, *Cowtown Columnist*, 4, 10, 11. Spectators were perched on piles of debris, they stood in the ruins of the building; they sat in windows surrounding the square. Thousands of eyes focused on the cornerstone from every direction.

— Jim Golden

Blair Cherry, who would later be the head coach of the University of Texas Longhorns, holds Rip not long after the toad was removed from the cornerstone of the old Eastland County courthouse.

The Decline
Of The Texas Horned Lizard

The horny toad population has fallen dramatically in the past half century, although belated protection was afforded by a statute forbidding their capture and sale. The reptile has almost disappeared from much of Texas. East of a line extending from Fort Worth to San Antonio to Corpus Christi they are seldom seen. Theories on the cause of their downfall vary. Zoologist Andrew Price, of the Texas Department of Parks and Wildlife, pointed to the invasion of fire ants:

> I think that in humans' efforts to combat the fire ant, they probably wipe out all ants, and since horned lizards are ant specialists, you wipe out their food. The problem with this explanation is that horned lizards are still occurring in areas where fire ants have already spread through, and they have also disappeared from areas where fire ants have not yet reached.[124]

Old Rip's fame constituted a major horned frog disaster. Tourists bought thousands as souvenirs and pets.

---

124 *Dallas Times Herald*, December 16, 1990.

Eastland filling stations gave them away as premiums. Delegates to the 1928 Democratic National Convention, in Houston, gladly paid $2.50 apiece for horny toads.[125] As they were misused, the Department of Agriculture warned of consequent serious damage to crops because of the proliferation of insects permitted by the reduced toad population.

Appalled by the destructive commerce, T. H. Scheffer wrote:

> The horned toad is quite gentle and inoffensive, often to its own undoing. For some tourists there are who appear to seek out in their peregrinations only the post card racks and convenient objects in Nature on which to carve their intitials. Such well meaning but thoughtless transients are too prone to buy from obtrusive vendors of souvenirs these little creatures of the desert, very useful at home as insect eaters but almost certain to perish from neglect or starvation when removed to unaccustomed surroundings. And the supply is not inexhaustible. Nature does not provide creature things in excess of balanced forces. So let us not waste her products.[126]

Perhaps as a gesture to Eastland tradition—or maybe to test and possibly break the record set by Old Rip—in 1928 a living horned frog was sealed inside the cornerstone of the present county courthouse; however, citizens who

---

125 House, *Cowtown Columist*, 7.
126 T. H. Sheffer, "Horned Toads," *Nature*, August 1930.

earlier had protested Rip's imprisonment would not permit a repetition of such cruelty. They petitioned the county commissioners to free the unfortunate tenant of the new building, and those enlightened public servants—recalling the criticism they and their predecessors had suffered over Rip's incarceration—liberated the toad.[127]

When Editor Boyce House learned that the occupant of the cornerstone was to be set free, he hurried to the square. After the toad was released, House dropped a newspaper into the cavity. He enjoyed imagining the consternation of those who—years later—would open the stone and discover a newspaper published one day after the stone was supposedly sealed. The lead story on the front page dealt with a frog that was left inside the stone, but there would be no trace of such a creature—dead or alive.[128]

Dennis Campbell, concerned about the demise of the little beasts, which were "a dime a dozen" when he was a boy, explained,

> The problem was that a market actually did exist for the lizards for many years, with Northerners taking the biological oddities back home as souvenirs. In the mid 1960s, though, legislation was enacted protecting these animals. But agricultural development and the incessant creeping of concrete across the land have taken their toll

---

127 "A whipped dog is a wiser dog." Emiliano Zapata, Mexican patriot.
128 House, *Cowtown Columnist*, 7.

as well. Gone are the days when one could readily find horned lizards in the yards and alleys of Texas cities. And even their rural brothers are no longer commonly encountered.[129]

When finally the State of Texas extended protection to the lizards, Joe Christie led the legislative effort.[130] Reporter Jimmy Banks described the incident that moved the senator to act:

A funny thing happened on a chiropractor's way to the forum recently and it resulted Wednesday in Sen. Joe Christie's introduction of a bill to protect horned toads. The chiropractor would have been better off with a frog in his throat than with one on his tie. He came to see the El Paso senator about a bill involving chiropractors and, while the two men were talking, Christie asked about his visitor's unusual tie clasp. It featured a small replica of a horned toad and the chiropractor explained that he owned an interest in a lucrative frog business. He also told Christie how the tie clasps are made.

"He said they take baby frogs," Christie recalled, "put them in a substance to form a mold and burn them to ashes. They remove the ashes and then just pour metal into the mold."

Christie was burned up about it. He began checking on the horned toad business and found that "hundreds of thousands of them are being shipped out of Texas for pets and curiosities. They go into a strange environment

---

129 Campbell, *Dallas Morning News*, "Backyard and Beyond."

130 Christie lived in Eastland before moving to El Paso.

up in the North or East and they die," said the senator. "One toad eats more than 40,000 insects a year—and the toads are absolutely harmless."[131]

Christie's bill provided for $200 fines and/or jail sentences of 10 to 60 days for violation of the statute, which made it "unlawful for any person to capture, trap, ensnare, willfully kill or injure, take or have in his possession for the purpose of sale, barter or commercial exploitation, horned toads . . . except for propagation and scientific purposes."[132]

Soon afterward the Texas House of Representatives approved a bill to protect the horned frog and the tortoise—two of the state's "biggest bug eaters." Sponsored by Rep. Neil Caldwell, of Angleton, the act imposed a fine but no jail time. (About 10,000 tortoises were sold each month by two Laredo firms, according to Curator Lawrence Curtis, of the Fort Worth Zoo.) Businesses selling the live reptiles as pets, and the dead as decorations, were targeted by the act, but their lobby persuaded representatives that men who captured and imprisoned horny toads and tortoises should not themselves be captured and imprisoned.[133]

131 Another authority claimed each consumed 70,000 insects annually.
132 *Dallas Morning News,* March 2 1967.
133 *Dallas Morning News,* May 15 1967.

The Texas Horned Lizard Conservation Society has made important contributions. Its sighting survey—asking Texans if they have seen a horned frog in the past decade—should focus attention upon the absence of those tiny companions of an earlier time and improve the chance of effective action.[134] The society intends to re-introduce the toads into their former domains; however, that is not possible where fire ants are plentiful. Spokesman Bill Davis wrote, "A horned lizard can eat 200 red ants a day. They can eat fire ants, too, but fire ants swarm them and kill them."[135]

---

134 The address of The Horned Lizard Conservation Society is Box 122, Austin, Texas 78767.

135 *Houston Chronicle*, August 20, 1992.

— Ann Huey-Bishop

Editor Boyce House was informed about the horned frog entombed in the courthouse cornerstone by the alleged perpetrator of the experiment to test the truth of the Texas belief that such a reptile could live a century in a vacuum. When the courthouse was slated for demolition, House wrote stories that were carried by newspapers all over the nation. On the day the cornerstone was opened, thousands were present to see what was or was not in the cavity.

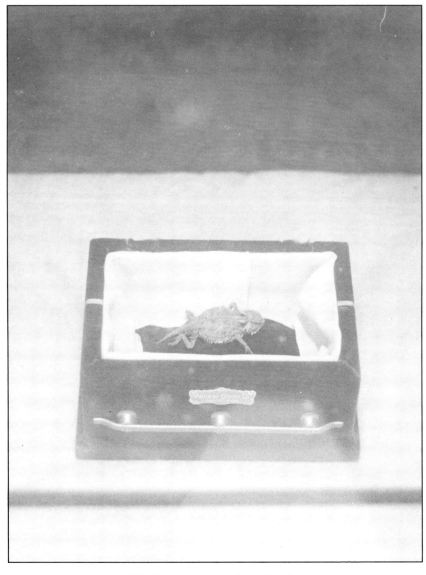

Rip (or an imposter) on display
in the Eastland County temple of justice.

Boyce House, Boswell To Old Rip

Eastland *Argus* editor Boyce House was the messenger who informed the world that three decades earlier a horny toad had been imprisoned in Eastland's courthouse and that the cornerstone in which it had been deposited was to be opened. That story launched House's career, in which he became a popular author of Texas books, a widely-read newspaper columnist, a radio personality, a poet, and, briefly, a candidate for high office.

House was born in Piggott, Arkansas on November 29, 1896 to newspaper editor Noah E. and Margaret O'Brien House. The family moved to Brownwood, Texas in 1905. After graduating from Central High School in Memphis, Tennessee, Boyce House, at nineteen, went to work for the *Commercial Appeal*.[136] He published the *Piggott Banner* before returning to Texas.

House edited the *Eastland Oil Belt News* and, at various times, newspapers in Brady, Ranger, Olney, and Cisco.[137] In addition to reporting, editing, and managing

---

136 *Dallas Journal*, July 1935.

137 H. V. O'Brien, Jr., *Old Rip, The Story of a Horned Toad That Slept for 30 Years*, Cisco, Texas: The Longhorn Press, 1965.

the business of the newpapers, House covered twenty-five football games each season. After working for the *Fort Worth Record* and the *Star-Telegram*, House was hired by Billy Rose to handle Casa Manana's publicity during the 1936 Texas Centennial celebration.

His experience in West Texas boomtowns generated by oil strikes furnished material for House's first book, *Were You In Ranger?* Metro-Goldwyn-Mayer retained him as technical adviser for the 1940 motion picture *Boom Town*, which was based upon the Burkburnett strike. The cast included Hollywood's major stars—Clark Gable, Spencer Tracy, Hedy Lamarr, Claudette Colbert, and Frank Morgan.[138]

In the 1930s House wrote and published poetry and his weekly column, "I Give You Texas," appeared in 200 newspapers. A quarter of a million Texans regularly listened to his radio broadcasts during the forties.

Although House covered Cisco's outrageous Santa Claus bank robbery and other important stories, his renown was based upon the Old Rip pieces of 1928. Commenting on the press coverage following demolition of the Eastland courthouse and discovery of the horned frog, House wrote,

138 *Who's Who in the South and Southwest*, 7th Edition, 1961. Steven H. Scheuer, *Movies on TV and Videocassette*, New York: Bantam Books, 1991, 117.

In newspaper space, Rip's total was exceeded only by the columns that Lindbergh had received for his hop across the Atlantic. Mark Twain's jumping frog became just an also-ran in public acclaim.

In 1942, House was stricken with a political fever and ran for public office. The biggest reputation in Texas politics at the time had been made wholly in radio. Governor Wilbert Lee "Pappy" O'Daniel had been the sales manager for Fort Worth's Burrus Milling Company when he hired Bob Wills and two other unemployed musicians to broadcast daily over KFJZ as the Light Crust Doughboys. As the program's announcer, O'Daniel attracted such a following that he would become the greatest vote-getter that Texas had known. By the time the United States entered World War II, O'Daniel was a senator, and radio personality Hal Collins was running for governor. House— perhaps counting upon name recognition from his newspaper and radio work—sought the Democratic nomination for lieutenant governor. He lost to John Lee Smith.[139]

Boyce House died in Fort Worth on December 30, 1961.[140] His books included:

---

139 Democrats so dominated Texas politics that their nomination was tantamount to election.

140 Eldon Branda, Ed. *The Handbook of Texas*, Austin: Texas State Historical Association, 1976, Vol. 3, 406.

Were You in Ranger? (1935)
Oil Boom (1941)
Texas Rhythm (1941)
I Give You Texas! (1941)
Tall Talk From Texas (1944)
Texas—Proud and Loud (1945)
Cowtown Columnist (1946)
Cub Reporter (1947)
Laugh Parade of States (1948)
City of Flaming Adventure (1949)
Texas Laughs and the Amazing Truth About Texas (1950)
Roaring Ranger, The World's Biggest Boom (1951)
Oil Field Fury (1954)
You Can Always Tell a Texan (1955)
Texas Treasure Chest (1956)
As I Was Saying (1957)
Friendly Feudin'—Alaska vs. Texas (1959)

Joe Chadwick, Goliad Martyr
And Admirer Of Horned Frogs

As George Catlin rode westward in 1834 with General Henry Leavenworth and Colonel Henry Dodge's First Dragoons, he was accompanied by an assistant. Joe Chadwick, born in New Hampshire in 1812, had been appointed to West Point and had resigned in 1831. Chadwick would help Catlin paint and document the western tribes of American Indians.[141]

By the time the command reached the Texas Panhandle, many soldiers were sick and some had died from exhaustion, bad water, and a malady that also killed the horses. Catlin was seriously ill.[142] From the bivouac in Texas designated as Camp Canadian, Catlin wrote:

> Six days of severe traveling have brought us from the Camanchee village to the North bank of the Canadian,

---

141 Attorney George Catlin gave up his Pennsylvania law practice in favor of painting the American Indians.

142 Of the 500 dragoons who rode westward in force to strike fear into the Plains Indians and persuade them to sign a peace treaty, only about 350 returned to Fort Gibson. Arrell M. Gibson, *Oklahoma, A History of Five Centuries*, Norman, Oklahoma: Harlow Publishing Corporation, 1965, 100.

where we are snugly encamped on a beautiful plain, and in the midst of countless numbers of buffaloes; and halting a few days to recruit our horses and men, and dry meat to last us the remainder of our journey.[143]

The plains around this, for many miles, seem actually speckled in distance, and in every direction, with herds of grazing buffaloes; and for several days, the officers and men have been indulged in a general license to gratify their sporting propensities; and a scene of bustle and cruel slaughter it has been, to be sure! From morning till night, the camp has been daily almost deserted; the men have dispersed in little squads in all directions, and are dealing death to these poor creatures to a most cruel and wanton extent, merely for the pleasure of destroying, generally without stopping to cut out the meat. During yesterday and this day, several hundreds have undoubtedly been killed, and not so much as the flesh of half a dozen used.

This poisonous and indigestible water, with the intense rays of the sun in the hottest part of the summer, is the cause of the unexampled sickness of the horses and men. Both appear to be suffering and dying with the same disease, a slow and distressing bilious fever, which seems to terminate in a most frightful and fatal affection of the liver.[144]

In these several cruel days' march, I have suffered severely, having had all the time (and having yet) a

---

143 Catlin, George, *Letters and Notes on the Manners, Customs, and Conditions of North American Indians*, New York: Dover Publications, 1973, Vol. II, 76.

144 Catlin, *Letters*, Vol. II, 77.

distracting fever on me. My real friend, Joe, has constantly rode by my side, dismounting and filling my canteen for me, and picking up minerals or fossils, which my jaundiced eyes were able to discover as we were passing over them; or doing other kind offices for me, when I was too weak to mount my horse without aid. During this march over these dry and parched plains, we picked up many curious things of the fossil and mineral kind, and besides them a number of the horned frogs. In our portmanteaux we had a number of tin boxes in which we had carried Seidlitz powders, in which we caged a number of them safely, in hopes to carry them home alive. Several remarkable specimens my friend Joe has secured of these, with the horns of half and three-fourths of an inch in length and very sharp at the points.

These curious subjects have so often fallen under my eye while on the Upper Missouri, that with me, they have lost their novelty in a great degree: but they have amused and astonished my friend Chadwick so much, that he declares he will take every one he can pick up, and make a sensation with them when he gets home. In this way Joe's fancy for horned frogs has grown into a sort of frog-mania, and his eyes are strained all day, and gazing amongst the grass and pebbles as he rides along, for his precious little prizes, which he occasionally picks up and consigns to his pockets.[145]

In the following year Catlin visited Chadwick in St. Louis and saw the toads "in their little tin boxes, in good flesh and good condition, where they had existed several months without food of any kind."

---

145 Catlin, *Letters*, Vol. II, 78.

Chadwick's horny toad enthusiasm during the 1834 expedition caused embarrassment after his discovery of another extraordinary frog. Catlin noted that:

> On one of these hard day's marches, and just at night whilst we were looking out for water, and a suitable place to encamp, Joe and I galloped off a mile or two to the right of the regiment, to a point of timber, to look for water, where we found a small and sunken stagnant pool; and as our horses plunged their feet into it to drink, we saw to our great surprise, a number of frogs hopping across its surface, as our horses started them from the shore!

> Several of them stopped in the middle of the pool, sitting quite "high and dry" on the surface of the water; and when we approached them nearer, or jostled them, they made a leap into the air, and coming down head foremost, went under the water and secreted themselves at the bottom.

> Here was a subject for Joe, in his own line! Frogs with horns, and frogs with webbed feet, that could hop about, and sit upon, the surface of the water!

> We rode around the pool and drove a number of them into it, and fearing that it would be useless to try to get one of them that evening we rode back to the encampment, exulting very much in the curious discovery we had made for the naturalists; and by relating to some of the officers what we had seen, got excessively laughed at for our wonderful discovery!

> Nevertheless, Joe and I could not disbelieve what we had seen so distinctly "with our own eyes"; and we took

to ourselves (or in other words, I acquiesced in Joe's taking to himself, as it was so peculiarly in his line) the most unequivocal satisfaction in the curious and undoubted discovery of this new variety; and we made our arrangements to ride back to the spot before "bugle call" in the morning; and by a thorough effort, to obtain a specimen or two of the web-footed frogs for Joe's pocket, to be by him introduced to the consideration of the knowing ones in the East.

Well, our horses were saddled at an early hour, and Joe and I were soon on the spot—and he with a handkerchief at the end of a little pole, with which he had made a sort of scoop-net, soon dipped one up as it was hopping along on the surface of the water, and making unsuccessful efforts to dive through its surface. On examining its feet, we found, to our very great surprise, that we had taken a great deal of pains to entrap an old and familiar little acquaintance of our boyhood; but, somewhat like ourselves, unfortunately, from dire necesssity, driven to a loathsome pool, where the water was so foul and slimy, that it could hop and dance about its surface with dry feet; and where it oftentimes found difficulty in diving through the surface to hide itself at the bottom.[146]

I laughed a great deal at poor Joe's most cruel expense, and we amused ourselves a few minutes about this filthy and curious pool, and rode back to the encampment. We found by taking the water up in the hollow of the hand, and dipping the finger in it, and drawing it over the side, thus conducting a little of it out; it was so slimy that the whole would run over the side of the hand in a moment!

146 Catlin, *Letters*, Vol. II, 79.

We were joked and teased a great deal about our web-footed frogs; and after this, poor Joe has had repeatedly to take out and exhibit his little pets in his pockets, to convince our traveling companions that frogs sometimes actually have horns.

In St. Louis, Catlin painted Joe Chadwick's portrait, which was to be sent to his mother, for he intended to volunteer to fight in the Texas Revolution.[147] Chadwick was with Colonel James Walker Fannin when they were captured by Mexican troops. Both were killed on March 27, 1836 in the massacre Santa Anna ordered for the helpless Goliad prisoners.[148]

---

147 I understand that the painting hangs in the old presidio at Goliad.

148 Webb, *Handbook of Texas*, Vol. 1, 325.

Sources

Newspapers and Magazines

Abilene Reporter-News, March 30, 1974.

Austin American-Statesman, September 30, 1930.

Brownwood Bulletin, March 1, 2, 10, 12, 1928.

Dallas Journal, July 1935.

Dallas Morning News, February 21-27, 1928; July 1, 14, 1928; January 20, 1929; July 22, 1951; January 18, 1964; March 2, 1967; April 5, 10, 1967; May 15, 1967; October 29, 1970; September 13, 1981; June 7, 1992.

Dallas Times Herald, February 19, 21, 22, 1928; March 3, 1968; January 16, 1990; December 16, 1990.

Fort Worth Record, February 24, 1928.

Houston Chronicle, August 20, 1992.

New York Times, May 3, 4, 6, 1928.

Time, May 30, 1927; August 8, 15, 1927; October 10, 1927.

Articles

Cochran, Doris, "When Is A Toad Not A Toad?" *Nature,* January 1932.

Ferguson, Gary, "There Are Horned Frogs — And There Are Horned Frogs," *TCU Monthly,* October 1975.

Goin, Jim, "Requiem or Recovery," *Texas Parks & Wildlife,* Vol. 50, No. 8, August 1992.

McAlister, Wayne, "Horned Symbol of Texas," *Texas Game and Fish,* 1953.

Potter, G.E., "Suffocation Point in the Horned Lizard, *Phrynosoma Cornutum,*" *Science,* Vol. 73.

Sheffer, T.H., "Horned Toads," *Nature,* August 1930.

Books

Branda, Eldon, Ed. *The Handbook of Texas,* Austin: The Texas State Historical Association, 1976, Vol. 3.

Catlin, George, *Letters and Notes on the Manners, Customs, and Conditions of North American Indians,* New York: Dover Publications, 1973, Vol. II.

Cox, Edwin T., *History of Eastland County,* San Antonio: Naylor Company, 1950.

Day, James M., *Black Beans and Goose Quills,* Waco: Texian Press, 1970.

Erath, George B., *The Memoirs of Major George B. Erath, 1813-1891,* Waco: The Heritage Society of Waco, 1956.

Ferrell, Robert H., Ed., *Dear Bess,* New York: W.W. Norton & Company, 1983.

Fryer, William T., *Readings on Personal Property,* St. Paul: West Publishing Company, 1938.

Garrett, Judith M. and Barker, David G., *A Field Guide to Reptiles & Amphibians of Texas*, Austin: Texas Monthly Press, 1987.

Ghormley, Pearl, *Eastland County, Texas,* Austin: Rupegey Publishing Company, 1969.

Gibson, Arrell M., *Oklahoma, A History of Five Centuries,* Norman: Harlow Publishing Corporation, 1965.

Hansen, Harry, Ed., *Texas, A Guide to the Lone Star State,* New York: Hastings House, 1969.

House, Boyce, *Cowtown Columnist,* San Antonio: Naylor Company, 1946.

Kinsella, W.P., *Shoeless Joe,* Boston: Houghton-Mifflin Publishing Company, 1982.

O'Brien, H.V., Jr., *Old Rip, The Story of a Horned Toad That Slept for 30 Years,* Cisco: Longhorn Press, 1965.

Presley, James, *A Saga of Wealth,* New York: G.P. Putnam's Sons, 1978.

Roemer, Ferdinand, *Texas*, San Antonio: Standard Printing Company, 1935, translated by Oswald Mueller.

First published in Bonn, this book was based upon the December 1845 to April 1847 visit of Dr. Ferdinand Von Roemer, a German lawyer and paleontologist, who surveyed the mineral resources of Texas.

Webb, Walter P., Ed., *The Handbook of Texas,* Austin: The Texas State Historical Association, 1952, Vol. 1.

West Texas Historical Association Yearbook, 1930.

Who's Who in the South and Southwest, 7th Edition, 1961.

Interviews and Letters

Golden, Jim, interview at his Eastland home on June 3, 1975.

Shelton, Myrtle Weems, Houston, letter to Elzina Prigmore Welch, Brownwood, October 9, 1992.

Wood, Mrs. Will, interview at her Abilene home on September 29, 1979.

Index